Praise for *Five Practices, Revised and Updated*

"One definition of genius is the ability to make complex things simple. Robert Schnase takes the complicated question of congregational purpose and effectiveness and creates a surprisingly accessible way to evaluate the health and vitality of your church. This updated edition of *The Five Practices* will both stimulate your thinking and offer immediately relevant practices that your church can use. Reading it alone, with your staff, or with your lay leadership team will lead to vibrant conversation and clearer ways to practice ministry in any context."

—Matt Miofsky, lead pastor, The Gathering, St. Louis, MO

"This book is rooted in deep faith in Jesus Christ and an unwavering hope for the church to be the church that God dreams of and that the world needs. Bishop Schnase integrates keen observation of our contemporary landscape with masterful storytelling and accessible application to bring true freshness and urgency to the Five Practices."

—Gregory V. Palmer, bishop, West Ohio Conference, UMC

"Bishop Schnase has given the church a great gift with his updated Five Practices of vital local churches. It will help the church function more faithfully and fruitfully in our present day."

—Jorge Acevedo, lead pastor, Grace Church, a multi-site
United Methodist Congregation, Southwest Florida

"The first edition of *Five Practices* was precisely what the church required at that time when congregations desperately needed a framework for moving activities and good intentions to transformed lives. That need remains, but the world has changed dramatically. This new edition addresses many of those changes with fresh perspectives and examples. Any congregation will benefit richly from this new version."

—Lovett H. Weems Jr., senior consultant, Lewis Center for Church
Leadership, Wesley Theological Seminary, Washington, DC;
coauthor, *Bearing Fruit: Ministry with Real Results*

"In 2007, we were enriched with Bishop Schnase's *Five Practices of Fruitful Congregations*. The book was received with wide acclaim around the world and included principles that energized and provided clarity to change lives for Jesus Christ. Bishop Schnase's new version shifts how we think about ministry and shows us how to go beyond the four walls of the traditional church. This reaches across denominations and will challenge all to put talents, gifts, and relationships to full use on Christ's mission field."

—Olu Brown, lead pastor, Impact Church, Atlanta, GA

"The Five Practices have had a profound influence on the ways we have created healthy and vital congregations over the past ten years. In this revision, Bishop Schnase has reflected on the transition from attractional to missional models of ministry, and how this shift expands our conceptions of discipleship and fruitfulness. With fresh language, clear thinking, and engaging narratives, Schnase's is a needed voice in a time of deep change."

—Kenneth H. Carter Jr., resident bishop, Florida Area, UMC;
coauthor, *Fresh Expressions: A New Kind of Methodist Church*

"Bishop Schnase is a voice to be listened to, as so many are learning. His critical thinking and practical application are a rare combination. This new book of the Five Practices is more than revised and updated. It is the product of continued learning, discernment, and experimentation. It models both mission and hope to leaders and congregations. Read it with others—then talk, pray, plan, and try."

—Gil Rendle, consultant and author

"This new resource is a must-have for every pastor, leader, and congregation. The book is full of practical application questions, innovative ideas and examples, and compelling guidance on how a church can live out the irresistible message and mission of Jesus in our world of today. It's a game-changer!"

—Sue Nilson Kibbey, director, Missional Church Consultation Initiative,
West Ohio Conference, UMC; author, *Flood Gates:
Holy Momentum for a Fearless Church*

Other Books by Robert Schnase

Just Say Yes! Unleashing People for Ministry
Seven Levers: Missional Strategies for Conferences
The Fruitful Living Series
Remember the Future: Praying for the Church and Change
Practicing Extravagant Generosity: Daily Readings on the Grace of Giving
Forty Days of Fruitful Living: Practicing a Life of Grace
Five Practices of Fruitful Living
The Balancing Act: A Daily Rediscovery of Grace
Cultivating Fruitfulness: Five Weeks of Prayer and Practice for Congregations
Five Practices of Fruitful Congregations
Ambition in Ministry: Our Spiritual Struggle with Success, Achievement, and Competition
Testing and Reclaiming Your Call to Ministry

Robert Schnase

Five Practices

of Fruitful Congregations

Revised and Updated

Abingdon Press™
Nashville

FIVE PRACTICES OF FRUITFUL CONGREGATIONS:
REVISED AND UPDATED

This book is printed on acid-free paper.

Library of Congress Cataloging-in-Publication Data has been requested.

978-1-5018-5887-1

18 19 20 21 22 23 24 25 26 27—10 9 8 7 6 5 4 3 2 1
MANUFACTURED IN THE UNITED STATES OF AMERICA

Contents

Acknowledgments

The encouragement of many friends has led to *Five Practices of Fruitful Congregations: Revised and Updated*. I'm thankful for rich discussions with Ray Altman, Laura Heikes, Karen Horan, Aaron Saenz, Mark Sheets, Ben Trammel, and Audrey Warren. Their insights and experiences shaped the new book considerably.

Conversation partners bring clarity, correction, and suggestion to my projects, and I particularly want to express my appreciation for Janice Huie, Gil Rendle, Ken Carter, Greg Palmer, Lisa Greenwood, Ruben Saenz, Alex Shanks, Lovett Weems, Cynthia Weems, and Judy Davidson. Without the steady hand, good advice, and frequent nudging of Connie Stella of Abingdon Press, I could not have completed this project. The behind-the-scenes support of Dalia Treviño has been essential. I could not offer a ministry of writing without the encouragement of my wife, Esther.

I'm indebted to the tens of thousands of Christian leaders who have used the original Five Practices material with their congregations, and then shared their stories with me and others over the years at workshops and conferences. Their experiences help me learn to teach and write in ways that are more helpful. Thank you.

My special appreciation goes to the Rio Texas Annual Conference of The United Methodist Church and to the pastors, everyday disciples, and congregations that continually surprise and delight me with creative and passionate approaches to ministry. I count it a privilege to serve alongside them in ministry. I give God thanks for all they do to offer the grace and peace of Christ in a broken world. May our work together be fruitful, and always to the glory of God.

—Robert Schnase

 *Introduction*

The Five Practices Revised and Updated

Radical Hospitality. Passionate Worship. Intentional Faith Development. Risk-Taking Mission and Service. Extravagant Generosity. People are searching for a church shaped and sustained by these qualities. The presence and strength of these five practices demonstrate congregational health, vitality, and fruitfulness. By repeating and improving these practices, churches fulfill their mission to make disciples of Jesus Christ for the transformation of the world.

The paragraph above opened the original *Five Practices of Fruitful Congregations*, published in 2007. No one imagined that in the years that followed, more than 600,000 copies of the book and its supplemental materials would strengthen thousands of congregations in multiple languages around the world. The practicality and simplicity of the ideas and the energizing quality of the adjectives that modify the practices have stimulated sermon series, leadership retreats, and discipleship discussions on six continents. The practices have brought clarity of purpose for Christian leaders and inspired boldness to initiate ministries that change lives. The Five Practices remain as fresh and as motivating today as when they first appeared in print.

And yet, when the original *Five Practices of Fruitful Congregations* was released, no one had iPhones, Facebook was limited to use by a few universities, Netflix mailed DVDs to our homes, and Blockbuster had over six thousand stores. Social media, in all its various expressions we know today, did not exist. The refugee crisis, the threat of terrorism in the US and Europe, the election of President Obama and then of President Trump, new conversations about race, gender, and guns in America, the changing attitudes toward immigrants—clearly, in our evolving world, so much has happened since the book was written.

The intervening years have also seen changes in our sense of community and how people regard institutions, including the church. Society has become more polarized. Cultural clashes have deepened. People select sources of news and information that reinforce their own points of view, insulating themselves from those who think differently. Many people are suspicious, resistant, or hostile toward the church while most are simply indifferent, viewing the church as irrelevant and unrelated to their lives. The "nones" (those people who check the "none" box on surveys of religious affiliation) have become larger than any particular faith expression. Because the composition of many churches does not match the ethnic, economic, or age demographics of the neighborhood where they are located, it's more important than ever for leaders of the church to ask, "Who is my neighbor?" Or more aptly, "Who is my neighbor *now*?"

As the culture has shifted since the original Five Practices, so has our understanding of church. Fruitful congregations are changing how they discern and organize their ministries. Leaders are experimenting with alternative models, with missional initiatives that reach the unchurched and the nominally churched by going to where the people are rather than expecting people to find a sanctuary and join in traditional church activities. Faith communities are experimenting with discipleship approaches that prepare people to take the ministry of Christ into their neighborhoods and work spaces rather than merely inviting people to come to their churches. Multicultural and next generation models are emerging that look completely different from what most church leaders have relied upon in the past. Fruitful ministries today are shifting from models based primarily on attractional assumptions (getting those outside the church to come to us) to models based more on missional assumptions (practicing discipleship that takes us into the places, communities, and networks people already inhabit).

Five Practices of Fruitful Congregations: Revised and Updated takes a fresh approach to the mission and practice of the church, shifting the focus from attractional assumptions to missional assumptions and providing a wealth of new examples from faith communities that are taking bold approaches to ministry. The revised and updated Five Practices has been prepared with the help of leaders on the cutting edge of ministry, benefiting from the experiments that have helped their faith communities reach new people with greater fruitfulness.

People know that the mission of the church is to make disciples of Jesus Christ, but they are seeking to understand how to fit this larger mission into their communities of faith in a practical way. These practices—Radical Hospitality, Passionate Worship, Intentional Faith Development, Risk-Taking Mission and Service, and Extravagant Generosity—are so critical to a congregation's purpose that failure to perform them in exemplary ways results in diminishing the church's mission. The evocative words used to express these qualities are irresistible because they move us from abstract intentions to practical and personal directions for ministry. Once our mission becomes practical and personal, it becomes memorable and achievable.

This book is designed to challenge leaders in holding a mirror to their own ministries to ask the questions, "How are we doing in practicing these qualities of ministry in our worship, music ministries, serving teams, study and support groups, mentoring programs, and leadership teams? How are we doing in our personal discipleship in our neighborhoods, workplaces, and the spaces where we engage friends and those we do not know?" The task of learning, deepening, repeating, and extending these practices should drive conversations about the work of the church, guide ministry teams, and shape planning and leadership training.

This book gives permission, focus, and encouragement for creative change and growth in ministry within the walls of the church and into the surrounding community by breaking down the universal mission of the church into achievable tasks and practical strategies. The Five Practices give leaders a common language that provides direction to everyone who belongs to the community about how to deepen their discipleship and extend the witness of the church. Faith communities become clear about their mission and confident about their future.

Every church exists in a wider community. People who live and work and go to school near our faith communities hunger for honest, healthy places to be and to belong. They yearn for others to respectfully demonstrate genuine interest and care. They long to welcome us into their lives and communities, and want us to graciously invite them into ours. They desire to experience God through authentic relationships, to find a place where it's safe to explore faith on their own terms and in their own languages, and to be part of a community where they can make a difference through service and generosity.

This book can be used to stimulate honest and positive conversations about your community of faith.

o   Plan a series of sermons, conversations, or dinner discussions, each based on one of these practices.

o   Invite ministry leaders to enter into significant dialogue about how God uses faith communities to form everyday disciples of Jesus Christ through these practices.

o   Allow these Five Practices to shape your own reflections about your area of ministry, and your personal discipleship.

Let these practices shape you and your faith community. Pray about them, mull them over, learn from them, amend them, deepen them, and elaborate on them so that we may all do our work more faithfully and fruitfully: the task of sharing the good news we have seen and known in Jesus Christ.

Chapter One

"Come and See" and "Go and Do"

"Welcome one another, therefore, just as Christ has welcomed you, for the glory of God." (Romans 15:7)

After this the Lord appointed seventy others and sent them on ahead of him in pairs to every town and place where he himself intended to go. (Luke 10:1)

First United Methodist Church in Miami, Florida, has been buffeted by the same forces that affect tens of thousands of congregations. Changing demographics, members moving farther away, ever-increasing facility costs that burden a decreasing and aging membership, thinning attendance patterns with regulars showing up one or two times a month instead of three or four times, difficulty with parking and playground space, declining visibility in the community—the list runs long. With each passing decade, attracting people to worship has become increasingly difficult. Even with excellent music and quality worship, fewer people made the drive or took the time to attend. As if drawing people who already belonged wasn't hard enough, attracting those who had no experience with any faith community or who harbored suspicion or mistrust about organized religion became nearly impossible.

While different in context and scope, the challenges of First UMC, Miami, match those of congregations large and small, in urban, suburban, and rural communities, and in every denomination. It's harder than ever to get people to respond to an invitation and make the effort to show up and worship with us in the church we love.

Adapting to the Context

Leaders of First United Methodist Church, Miami, knew things had to change or they would fail in their fundamental mission. Pastor Audrey Warren and her predecessor, Cynthia Weems, worked with the congregation to dramatically reshape their approach to ministry. The people in the congregation learned, over the course of a few years, that in order to fulfill their mission they must adapt their ministries to the new context of their community. They began to "go and do," actively engaging with the people who live and work in their area. They stepped back to examine their habits of worship and saw ways to reconceive it, to worship with new expressions, to engage and include new people. They deepened their commitment to homeless people in their community and formed partnerships with businesses in order to meet basic human needs. They worked with a developer to rethink their use of space and facility. In these and other remarkable ways, First UMC's leaders and faithful people found the courage and energy to adopt a more experimental approach toward ministry. A few examples help to tell the story:

Leaders in the congregation decided to become more intentional about engaging the downtown business community, looking for potential alliances with other groups who shared a commitment to improving life for people in the area. Along the way, as part of the congregation's effort to adapt ministries to their context, the church decided to forego a traditional Maundy Thursday service and instead offer a foot washing experience for homeless people. Was it awkward at first? Perhaps, but it became a Saturday event that involves hundreds of people. First UMC's leaders used this foot washing service, which honors the act of service

Jesus offered to his disciples at the Last Supper, as a starting point for other experimental initiatives.

The congregation forged an alliance with Barry University in Miami, which happens to run a podiatry program. Podiatry students and faculty are invited to share in ministry by tending to the physical needs of each person at the foot washing. Another partner, *Soles for Souls*, provides a pair of shoes for each homeless guest at the event. The foot washing ministry continues to be a signature piece of First UMC's vision for downtown, reflecting the role of the church as servant to the community. An invitation to serve and to form relationships with the homeless has been the primary entryway for many people who now belong to the congregation.

People want to do something that matters and belong to a church that makes a difference. The foot washing relieves suffering, offers hope and connection, and forms relationships. It provides a channel for those who want to make a difference to put faith into action. Many folks who would never think to attend a worship service, including several podiatry students and business partners, gladly offer themselves to help with this ministry of Christ for the poor.

Another example of First UMC's reshaped approach to ministry involves peanut butter and jelly. People who are homeless are often also hungry, so leaders in the congregation approached local businesses to ask if their employees would like to make sandwiches for homeless people. First Church provides the ingredients, and employees willingly give up their lunch break to make sandwiches. People from the congregation go to the office buildings, becoming the guests in their space, serving side by side with downtown workers to address an unmet community need. The ministry forms relationships of mutual trust, friendship, and partnership between those who worship in a church downtown and those who work in office buildings nearby.

Yoga Chapel, another ministry of First UMC, engages people who otherwise might never be inclined to sit in a pew or participate in traditional worship services. Services weave together the art of Christian storytelling and meditation with the wisdom of yoga practice, providing a time to attend to spiritual, physical, and relational well-being through scripture, conversation, music, and prayer that connects people to God and one another. The ministry uses the affinity networks that already exist among those who practice yoga.

Through such innovative approaches to ministry, First UMC has arrested decline and multiplied the points of contact and the impact of its ministry. The congregation has made substantial progress in reaching its neighborhood. While it remains an unfinished story, First United Methodist Church has become clearer about its mission and more confident about its future.

Attractional Models

In the original *Five Practices of Fruitful Congregations*, most ideas for increasing fruitfulness relied upon attractional assumptions. Churches that practice radical hospitality "take the initiative to invite, welcome, include, and support newcomers." The book describes hospitality as "the active desire to invite, welcome, receive and care for those who are strangers" (p. 11).

These words assume that the critical activities that we should work on are those that improve our welcoming skills, enhance our worship services, and strengthen our small-group ministries so that people will be attracted to us, join us in our activities, and become members of our congregations.

In the years since the original book, fruitful congregations have discovered that while *attractional models* are helpful and necessary to fulfill the mission of Christ, they simply are not enough. Faith communities must also develop ministries that derive from *missional assumptions*, activities that primarily benefit people who are not members of the church, often in places far away from church facilities. These ministries require a different posture toward our neighborhoods, a more deliberate outward focus, and a willingness to carry Christ's love to where people already live, work, and play rather than hoping for people to come to us.

Hospitality doesn't stop with merely inviting people to come to our churches and to like what we like and do what we do. It involves opening ourselves to the mission of Christ, to the possibility that we are being sent by God into the neighborhoods where we live and the gatherings to which we belong. Radical hospitality even nudges us to form relationships of mutual respect and service among people who live in circumstances considerably different from our own, to befriend strangers in order to offer the grace and love of God.

An ever-increasing number of people in our communities will never step through a church door. "Nones" and "dones" outnumber people in any other religious category. "Nones" are people who check the none box on surveys about religious affiliation, and "dones" are those who are finished with all things related to the institutional church because of the scandals, exclusionary practices, or irrelevance of the church to their lives. If we merely wait for people to visit us, we surrender any hope of sharing the love of Christ with the majority of the people around us.

Does the description of "nones" and "dones" bring people you know to mind?

One couple who belong to a church that offers compelling worship asked their neighbors if they would attend worship with them. The neighbors had zero interest in going to church and had nothing positive to say about institutional religion. And yet, those same neighbors showed an eagerness to join with the couple and other neighbors for dinner conversations about faith, the spiritual life, and serving others. Their dinners became an expression of Christ's community in their home, among people who would never think to show up for a Sunday morning worship service in a sanctuary.

What We Hope Happens

Why do we assume that people who do not know our congregation will one day find themselves as a member of our church? How do we think it happens?

Most congregations, consciously or unconsciously, operate with attractional assumptions. They imagine that a person, a couple, or a family becomes aware of their church, perhaps through the invitation of a friend, an advertisement on a billboard, or by driving past the sanctuary.

5

Churches then hope that what the new persons hear or see will draw them toward the congregation. They assume that the visitors will share a common interest in the purpose of the church or feel a desire to form an affinity with the church. A yearning to learn, grow spiritually, belong, and serve will cause them to visit and will lead them to greater participation.

The church assumes that some newcomers will find the congregation so appealing that they willingly overcome any hesitancies they may feel about entering unfamiliar space with unfamiliar people and unfamiliar habits. With ever-increasing experience with the church, the newcomers will feel they belong, strengthen their faith commitments, and become members in order to benefit from the church's ministries and support its mission. The church woos them to deeper relationship and surrounds them with the grace of God.

To summarize, the system by which most churches seek to grow goes something like this: We hope and pray that twelve new Christian households move into our neighborhood next year. And we hope that at least eight of those find our church and visit our worship service. And of those eight, we assume six will like us enough to return, and that four will officially become members. We believe that with a passionate congregation, those outside the church will hear about the church, believe that things are different or better with this church, and then come.

We never articulate this as our plan, but when we rely entirely upon attractional assumptions, this is our system for reaching people who do not know Christ.

How closely do the paragraphs above describe how we assume people come to belong to our church? How well does this approach work for reaching the "nones" and "dones"?

We assume this pathway for entry into the church because it matches the experience of many people who currently belong. Attractional models worked in the past when the culture expected people to attend worship and people wanted to be members of churches. We still take it for granted that this is how the church grows, even though this approach stopped working long ago.

Many of the attractional assumptions we rely upon to reach new people are no longer true. What happens when people no longer trust institutions in general nor the church in particular? Or when next generations don't share a taste for the style of music that we offer in worship and don't appreciate the one-way verbal communication of a sermon? *Becoming a member* of anything is unappealing to many people and does not motivate them to deepen their spiritual lives. They are not seeking to *join* anything. Many churches are surrounded by neighbors who speak a different language or who are of a different ethnicity than the majority in the congregation. What would cause them to show up for worship?

What happens when generations of people living around us have no experience with worship, no vocabulary for understanding faith, no familiarity with scripture, and have never once stepped inside a church? The culture provides an ever-increasing number of competing activities on Sundays that are more compelling than church attendance. Our assumptions no longer serve us well. *The way we've always done it* doesn't work in a context where most young adults believe the church is boring, judgmental, hypocritical, out of touch, anti-homosexual, insensitive, old-fashioned, and boring. (See *unChristian: What a New Generation Really Thinks about Christianity* by David Kinnaman and Gabe Lyons [Baker Books, 2012].)

When people do not find the idea of church appealing, they are not attracted to what we do, no matter how well we do it.

Come and See & Go and Do

In the Gospel of John, Jesus and his earliest followers repeat the invitation, "Come and see." Their approach is invitational, and at various times, hundreds of people gather to listen to Jesus's teachings.

In a similar way today, the compelling nature of the gospel and the openness and friendliness of the congregation exert an influence that pulls people toward Christ and prompts them to make decisions about life and faith. Come and see!

Ministries based on attractional assumptions are necessary and important. Congregations depend upon attractional assumptions to fulfill the mission of Christ.

And yet Jesus does not sit passively waiting for people to come to him. It isn't just in the synagogue that Jesus offers God's radical hospitality. *Jesus was seldom in the same place for long.* Jesus's life-changing encounters happen while Jesus is on the move, in the real places where he engaged people, in their houses, at their dinner tables, in their grain fields, in their fishing boats. He listens and teaches as they mend nets, trade in the marketplace, walk beside the sea, move through crowded streets, journey along the road. He meets people right where they are, literally and metaphorically, engaging them where they actually live and work and also wherever they are spiritually. He practices hospitality, while he himself had no place to call home.

Jesus stepped into the lives of people of all types, Jews and Gentiles, women and men, neighbors and strangers, the up-and-coming, and the down-and-out even though his disciples often tried to restrain him from doing so. He crossed borders, literally and figuratively—speaking to the woman at the well despite her being a foreigner, dining with tax collectors even though they were considered traitors, healing on the Sabbath over the objections of the Pharisees, intervening on behalf of the woman accused of adultery at the risk of his own life. None of these people were ever going to show up at a synagogue to listen to his teaching. Most were prohibited from doing so, by religious law or because of the ostracism of religious leaders. Jesus stepped toward those who were different from him. His ministry was on the road, an itinerant conveyer of the grace of God.

Jesus welcomed the stranger, but he also became the stranger who accepted the welcome of others to offer them God's grace.

To focus on the missional aspects of our work rightly pushes us beyond the notion that we fulfill our task when we pour all our efforts into making a congregation so attractive to unchurched people that they will come to their senses, show up in our place of worship, fall in love with music we like, and agree to our way of doing things. It breaks through our passivity by pointing us to the active verbs of the gospel of Jesus Christ:

Go . . . Tell . . . Teach . . . Pray . . . Give . . . Heal . . . Love . . . Forgive . . . Baptize . . . God's grace compels us to go places we might never go if left to our own preference and convenience. In a broken world, no church can sit still when drawn into the mission of Christ. A missional focus gives the church an ever-restless quality, pushing us outward into the world and among the people who are so loved by God that he gave his only son.

Imagine what ministry might look like that goes to every place where Jesus himself intends to go!

This Way *and* That Way

A friend gave me a six-inch heavy ceramic ampersand. An ampersand is the squiggly figure that looks like this: &. It simply means *and*. An ampersand binds two ideas together in a sentence or on a sign. I keep the ampersand in a visible place in my office to remind myself that when I'm trying to decide to *either* choose one way of doing things or another way, that I should consider how I can do things *both* this way *and* that way.

Working with missional assumptions and attractional assumptions is not an either/or choice. Healthy, fruitful, growing congregations seek to do both with excellence. They work to improve their invitation and welcome. And they work to extend their sending and outreach. To do either well requires the practices of radical hospitality, passionate worship, intentional faith development, risk-taking mission and service, and extravagant generosity.

The same skills are needed to offer ministries that welcome people into our community as well as ministries that take the love of Christ into other spaces: the ability to listen, to learn, to prepare, to share the grace of God and offer the embrace of Christ. But the two approaches require different strategies of initiative, planning, and intentionality. Both approaches are undergirded by prayer and by an authentic desire for what is best for the spiritual and temporal well-being of those persons God entrusts to us to share the love of Christ.

These two approaches are highlighted throughout *Five Practices of Fruitful Congregations: Revised and Updated*. Every chapter includes examples of ministries based on attractional assumptions and those based on missional models. The first involves opening our doors for others to enter into our spaces, networks, communities, and facilities to become part of our worshipping communities, support groups, studies, and service ministries. The second involves moving away from where we are and stepping out through our doors into the communities and networks of others in order to form relationships and connect with them.

Each of the Five Practices remains effective and essential regardless of whether attractional or missional assumptions primarily drive the work of a particular ministry.

These are two necessary tasks of discipleship—welcome the stranger and take the love of God with us into other communities where God sends us.

Welcoming Newcomers & Becoming Guests

"Why don't those people come to church?" This often-repeated question expresses the frustration that a small congregation felt about the people who lived in the trailer park next door. Church members made several efforts to invite and welcome, but nothing worked. Then a few members took Crock-Pots of food to the trailer park and started to share meals with the residents. This led to deeper conversations. The folks from the church listened and learned and came to know the people. As time went on, they added time for prayers and singing. They learned about the conditions that their low-income neighbors lived with, and this inspired the church to build restrooms for the residents. The church eventually built a small amphitheater and offered worship in the trailer park. More than seventy people regularly attend.

To reach the people in the trailer park required that everyday disciples reconceptualize their mission. Was their primary goal to get people to come to their sanctuary and join them in their church? Or was it to form relationships with people for the love of Christ wherever that might take place? Was it to make people into members of a church or to form people into followers of Christ?

The Crock-Pot Ministry continues to bear fruit as lives are changed by the grace of God. Through countless shared dinners and attentive conversations, the church earned the right to offer worship where residents live.

A strategy based only on attractional assumptions would never have worked.

The challenge is not merely how to do better at welcoming the newcomer into our space by improving signage and parking, increasing accessibility, training greeters, following up with guests, and assimilating them into our community, but also how we become newcomers ourselves in other places in order to listen, learn, connect, serve, and share the grace of God with people who might never be inclined to enter our facilities or worship at our services. When we allow the Holy Spirit to push us beyond "come to us" thinking, we begin to imagine "go to them" possibilities for all the places we can carry the grace of God with us to where people already gather.

What community of people near your church causes you to ask, "Why don't those people come to our church?" Have you wondered what "going to them" would look like?

Third Places

Nearly thirty years ago, the sociologist Ray Oldenburg developed the concept of third places. Third places are gathering points where we spend time with others in community, beyond the social environments of the first two places where we spend most of our time, at home and work. Third places foster our sense of belonging, our connection to others, our identity, and our sense of responsibility toward others. Such places are essential for social cohesion, knitting us together into a community, interweaving the threads of our individual lives into the fabric of society. In decades past, a primary third place in most communities was the church.

In his book *The Great Good Place: Cafes, Coffee Shops, Bookstores, Bars, Hair Salons, and Other Hangouts at the Heart of a Community* (Marlowe and Company, 1989), Oldenburg describes several key characteristics of these third places: there are no economic barriers to entrance; there is food and drink; the space is highly accessible; there are regulars, who are usually present, and newcomers, who are welcomed and received with ease; there is a quality of neutral space; the dominant mode of communication is conversation; and the mood is playful.

Think about how many churches fail to fulfill these basic characteristics. Too many congregations provide a sense of welcome for one social class but not another, or their space is not physically (or relationally) accessible. Some churches make newcomers feel like outsiders forever or foster an atmosphere that is far from playful.

Third places include coffee shops, fitness centers, sport leagues, computer gaming places, bars, bowling alleys, dog parks, neighborhood associations, running groups, country clubs, yoga studios, online communities, hiking trails, libraries, community centers, and meeting places of hobbyists of various sorts, including birders, quilters, gardeners, fishing enthusiasts, photographers, bikers, blacksmiths, and those who participate in service organizations, resort communities, renaissance fairs, orchestras, community chorales, martial arts studios, and places where people share a common interest in the environment and in improving literacy for children.

Third places are where people know one another and welcome one another by name. They foster rich relationships that begin with a common connecting interest or affinity. We in the church have not used the idea of third places well. We tend to think about how to make our church feel more like a third place by adding a coffee bar in the church entryway rather than meeting people in their third space where they naturally gather.

Many people reading this book not only belong to a faith community but also to one or more such affinity groups. Ministry based upon missional assumptions means we see ourselves as belonging to these gatherings for a purpose. God has prepared us, equipped us, and sent us into these networks with the purpose of carrying with us the grace of Christ. Without a preachy, knows-all-the-answers, intrusive attitude, but with a spirit of humility, of attentiveness, of listening and learning and serving, we ask God to use us for God's purposes among those we know and love and among the strangers with whom God brings us into contact.

What third places in your community come to mind as you read this? Where have you formed relationships and come to know people outside of church and work?

Where we live is more than a geographical accident, and the networks we belong to are more than a happenstance of common interests. The idea that we are being sent by God helps us understand what it means to intentionally structure ministries based on missional assumptions.

The New Five Practices

Those familiar with the original *Five Practices of Fruitful Congregations* will notice considerable differences that distinguish this *Revised and Updated Edition* from the earlier book.

In the new book, Radical Hospitality is not merely focused on getting people to come to church. Rather, we think about how we carry hospitality with us with greater intentionality into our neighborhoods, work life, and affinity networks. What good is Christian hospitality if it's something we only practice for an hour on Sunday morning while failing to form relationships with the people who live next door?

Passionate Worship in the new book extends beyond improving what happens on Sunday morning in the sanctuary. Worship becomes mobile, portable, on the move, going to where people live and work and play.

The practice of Intentional Faith Development includes more focus on experiential learning, mentoring, spiritual formation, and forming relationships in addition to traditional content-based education in Bible studies and Sunday school classes.

Risk-Taking Mission and Service in the new edition explores relationships more deeply and offers examples to shift from doing *ministry for* to less patronizing, more relational models of doing *ministry with* those who suffer hardship or injustice.

The chapter on Extravagant Generosity uses fresh examples that help people learn to love generosity as a way of life.

A Significant Shift

Five Practices of Fruitful Congregations: Revised and Updated shifts how we think about ministry.

Come to us ideas are balanced with *Go to them* initiatives. Strategies for *doing things better* are strengthened with ideas for *doing things differently.* *Teaching people to do things our way* is intermixed with *learning new things from others. Doing ministry for* becomes *doing ministry with.*

Welcoming the guest expands to *becoming a newcomer* among others. *Increasing activities in the church* shifts toward *offering ministries beyond our facilities. Making our church more interesting to others* expands to *becoming more interested in the spiritual needs and real-life issues of others.*

Receiving people in the spirit of Christ expands to *being sent to the people around us in the spirit of Christ. Come and See* becomes *Go and Do.*

The original *Five Practices* book gave responsibility to everyday disciples for the ministry of the church rather than focus on just the pastor or the formal leadership teams.

Five Practices of Fruitful Congregations: Revised and Updated takes things a step further by exploring more deeply what it means to see each one of us as disciples, as called and sent by God, so that the good news of Christ's love penetrates into the places and spaces, networks and neighborhoods, affinity groups and relationships we already inhabit as well as into new places we've never been before. The Five Practices help us understand ourselves as responsible for carrying the love of Christ into every place we go, with intentionality, grace, and humility.

A More Expansive View

We began the chapter with the example of First United Methodist Church, Miami. As the church adapted to the changing context of ministry, leaders also remained attentive to the quality of current ministry, including Sunday morning worship, an excellent music ministry, small group studies, and long-term missional commitments. Wisely, they never abandoned ministries based on attractional assumptions. Rather, they shifted the mix of approaches from perhaps 80 percent attractional and 20 percent missional to something closer to 50 percent attractional and 50 percent missional.

The purpose of the new Five Practices is to present ideas, examples, and models that help congregations make a similar shift. *Five Practices of Fruitful Congregations: Revised and Updated* stirs conversation and stimulates rethinking so that churches that have unconsciously operated with inherited assumptions can begin to take a more expansive view of ministry and more intentionally form relationships with those outside the walls of the church.

The shift of energy, focus, and imagination is life-giving. This is an exciting time to offer ourselves to ministry, as pastors and everyday disciples. The spaces and contexts in which we serve demand infinitely more creativity, a taste for trying new things rather than merely doing what we've always done before. The current reality requires a more permission-giving, experimental temperament that unleashes people for ministry. When the church leaves the building to offer ministries that matter, we view ourselves as part of Christ's mission in a whole new way, as sent into a mission field uniquely prepared by God that uses the talents, gifts, and relationships God has given us.

Chapter Two

The Practice of Radical Hospitality

"I was a stranger and you welcomed me." (Matthew 25:35)

A young woman stands awkwardly in the church's foyer with her toddler, looking around at all the people she does not know. An acquaintance at work casually mentioned how she loved the praise band at her church and invited the woman to visit, but now she is not so sure this was a good idea. She is self-conscious about the fussiness of her little one, unsure where the bathroom is, too timid to ask directions, doubting whether this is the right worship service for her, or whether this is even the right church. Except for a funeral and a couple of weddings, she's never been inside a church. Where is she to sit, what is it going to feel like to sit alone with her child, and what if her baby makes too much noise? She feels the need for prayer, for some connection with others, and for something to lift her above the daily grind of her job, the unending bills, the conflicts with her ex-husband, and her worries for her child, but visiting a church for the first time feels daunting. Being the stranger among people who already know one another is unnerving.

Now, imagine what would happen if the people of the congregation took Jesus's words seriously when he said, "I was a stranger and you welcomed me . . ." They would see this woman and the whole bundle of hopes and anxieties, desires and discomforts that she carries, and think, "She belongs to Jesus's family, and Jesus wants us to treat her as we would treat Jesus himself if he were here." With this in mind, what would be the quality of the welcome, the efforts to ease the awkwardness? What would be the eagerness to listen to her and learn about the life she lives and the things that matter most to her? What would be the enthusiasm to help, to serve, to graciously encourage her? Taking Jesus seriously leads us to practice radical hospitality.

Christian Hospitality

Vibrant, fruitful, growing congregations practice Radical Hospitality. Out of genuine love for Christ and for others, they take the initiative to invite, welcome, and include newcomers and help them grow in faith as they become part of the body of Christ. They focus on those beyond their congregation with as much passion as they attend to the nurture and growth of those who already feel connected, and they apply their utmost creativity, energy, and effectiveness to the task, exceeding all expectations.

The roots of the word *hospitality* originally meant serving as a good host as well as being a good guest. The Latin *hospes* meant both *host* and *guest*, and is derived from *hosti*, which means *enemy* (think hostile!) and *poi*, which means *people*. Whether you were a guest among strangers or were welcoming a stranger as a guest in your space, hospitality came to mean engaging strangers with goodwill, overcoming the estrangement, the distance, the unknown with a receiving, open spirit.

Christian hospitality reveals a genuine love for others, an outward focus, a reaching out to those not yet known, a grace that motivates people to openness and adaptability, a willingness to change behaviors to accommodate the needs and receive the talents of newcomers. It describes the active desire to invite, welcome, receive, and care for those who are strangers so that they find a spiritual home and discover for themselves the unending richness of life in Christ. Hospitality brings the heart of God into view through us.

Hospitality also describes the yearning to be *sent* by Christ into the lives of others to share the gracious love of Christ in whatever circumstance we find ourselves. Radical hospitality respects the dignity of others, and expresses God's initiating and inviting love for every person. It is a mark of Christian discipleship, a quality of Christian community, a concrete expression of commitment to grow in Christ-likeness by seeing ourselves as belonging to the community of faith "not to be served but to serve" (Matthew 20:28). As we practice hospitality, we become part of God's invitation to abundant life. It is Christ's welcome, not merely our own, that we offer others.

Grounded in Christ

Hospitality streams through scripture, with both its attractional and missional aspects, and it's grounded in God's revelation in Jesus Christ.

In Deuteronomy, God reminds the people of Israel to welcome the stranger, the sojourner, the wanderer. Why? "For you were strangers in the land of Egypt" (Deuteronomy 10:19).

We, too, were once estranged from God, strangers to the faith, residing outside the community where we now find rich resources of meaning, grace, hope, friendship, and service. We belong to the body of Christ because of someone's hospitality. Someone invited us or reached out to us, encouraged us, offered us the embrace of Christ. Someone—a parent, a spouse, a friend, a pastor, or even a stranger—helped us feel that we belonged to God. We were engrafted into the body of Christ. If we had not felt accepted, loved, welcomed, and supported in some measure, we would not have remained connected.

At every turn, the disciples seem ready to draw boundaries and distinctions that keep people at a distance from Jesus. They have a thousand reasons to ignore, avoid, and thwart the approach of people, reminding Jesus that some of these people are too young, too sick, too sinful, too Roman, too blind, or too Gentile to deserve his attention. Jesus teaches, "Whoever welcomes one such child in my name welcomes me" (Matthew

18:5). In every instance, Jesus radically challenges the disciples' expectations by overstepping boundaries to invite people toward him.

Jesus not only invited people into his life, he also lived with such authentic compassion that people invited him into their places. He dined with tax collectors and sinners, whom everyone else avoided. He approached the woman at the well with such grace that she did not turn away. Rather, she talked with him and listened to him. Jesus stepped toward people others stepped away from: the blind, the sick, the paralyzed, the grieving, those with unclean spirits. He didn't wait for people to find him; he searched for and found them, and accepted their hospitality while offering his own. He entered into their lives, and then into their hearts. He welcomed strangers, and became the stranger welcomed into households, dinner parties, wedding feasts, and everyday conversations.

Christian hospitality has us seeing people as Jesus sees them and seeing Jesus in the people God brings us into contact with.

Biblical Hospitality and the Early Church

The Apostle Paul implores the followers of Christ to practice an active hospitality. "Welcome one another, therefore, just as Christ has welcomed you, for the glory of God" (Romans 15:7). The grace received in Christ places upon Christians the joyful gift and challenging task of offering others the same welcome they themselves have received in Christ.

The Letter to the Hebrews cautions, "Do not neglect to show hospitality to strangers, for by doing that some have entertained angels without knowing it" (Hebrews 13:2). The people we befriend often prove to be those through whom God graces us. Churches change when they form relationships with newcomers and accept their spiritual gifts and faith experiences. Ministry expands. God uses newcomers to breathe new life into communities of faith.

Paul allowed himself to be shaped and formed by the communities he reached with God's grace. "I have become all things to all people, that I might by all means save some" (1 Corinthians 9: 22). He did not disguise who he really was. But he was willing to adapt himself to varying contexts to listen, learn, and appreciate those who did not feel they belonged to God's family.

The tenth chapter of Acts describes the conversion of Cornelius, a Gentile, who follows a vision from God by welcoming Peter into his home. More important, the story details a conversion for Peter, his opening himself to possibilities he never before imagined. Peter steps into Cornelius's house, full of strangers that religious law restricts Peter from mixing with, and he eats with them, converses with them, listens to their dreams. The Holy Spirit works through Peter and he realizes that these persons, Gentile and unclean, are worthy of his focus and time, and that they, too, are recipients of God's redeeming love. Peter sees his hosts differently, and this mutual hospitality, offered and received, changes the course of Christianity.

Hospitality and Early Methodism

John Wesley and the early Methodists practiced hospitality in ways so radical in their day that many traditional church leaders found their activities offensive. Wesley preached to thousands on roadsides and in open fields in order to reach coal miners, field laborers, factory workers, the underclass, and the poorest of the poor. He invited them into a way of life and nurtured in them a strong sense of belonging as he organized societies and classes for mutual accountability, support, and care. Wesley taught of God's prevenient grace: the preceding, preparing grace that opens people to God.

According to Wesley, before people ever consciously come to faith, they have inner desires for relationship to God that are stifled, forgotten, neglected, ignored, or denied. By the grace that precedes awareness or decision, God creates readiness for faith and fosters the nascent eagerness to please God. By God's grace, people may be more ready than we realize to accept the initiative of Christ. Just as God's prevenient grace enables people to move closer to God, so also God's grace works through the church to offer relationships with others and with God. God's grace activates interest and eagerness for relationship in the individual just as God's grace uses the invitational posture and outward focus of faith communities to reach out in love.

Wesley broke out of the constraints of the institution of the church when he experimented with preaching outdoors to the crowds gathering before and after work instead of confining himself to the pulpits of churches. His emerging awareness of God's call resulted not merely in a change of heart, but of location, of place, as he opened himself to being sent. He stepped away from the academic cloisters and the Church of England pulpits into the open fields. He moved beyond the homes of priests and professors and into the homes of the poor. He crossed social and economic borders to learn about the daily lives of people who did not enjoy his privilege and status. Because of this, God helped Wesley see the world differently. He realized the mission field was changing, and a singular focus on parish churches would no longer be sufficient. He trained his eyes to willfully observe the people whom the established church barely noticed.

Communities of faith that practice radical hospitality willfully see people most churches barely notice. Ministries based on missional assumptions rescue us from preoccupation with ourselves and reorient us toward our neighbor and toward the transformation of the world. An outward focus appropriately highlights the "sentness" of Christian disciples, and reaffirms that God uses us as ambassadors of Christ, making his appeal through us. Radical hospitality means little when we only practice it for an hour each week to welcome newcomers to our worship services if we don't even know the people who live next door to us and fail to practice the hospitality of Christ in our daily encounters.

The Learning Congregation

Leaders of a congregation wanted to deepen their understanding of hospitality, growing beyond the practical steps recommended by books on church growth. They had the techniques right—helpful signage, accessible parking, trained greeters, and a system for following up with guests. Now they sought a culture of hospitality that extended into all discipleship classes, mission projects, music teams, and youth ministries. The pastor invited ten people to a series of lunches for in-depth study and reflection on welcoming people into the body of Christ. These people loved the church, lived the faith, and were those whom others naturally followed. They arranged their work schedules and family responsibilities to attend for an hour and a half, once a week, for six weeks.

In the first session, they shared how each of them had come to be a part of the body of Christ. They discussed questions such as, "Who first invited us or brought us to church? Who reached out to us and made the life of faith appealing? How did we become more involved, and what ministry did we first participate in? What made us feel like we belonged? What difficulties did we have to overcome?" They talked about people, places, services, relationships, pastors, and studies that God used to draw them in and form them into disciples. Some remembered making attempts to enter faith communities where they felt resistance, obstacles, coldness. Next, they talked about what had brought each one into relationship with the church to which they currently belonged. How had they first heard about the church? What was their first experience like? What made them feel welcome, or what made it hard to connect? Many were surprised to hear how difficult it had been for some people to feel warmly embraced. Others reminisced about particular people who encouraged them. It was an honest and profoundly moving conversation, intermingling the experiences of long-term members with those who had recently become part of the faith community.

During another session, the leaders delved into the theological meaning of the church as the body of Christ and the "why" of hospitality. They discussed the purpose for which the church exists—to draw people into relationship with God through Jesus Christ—and how this changes lives. To live in community with others is part of God's plan. A faith community is *a school for love*, the place where God's Spirit forms us and where we learn to give love to and receive love from friends, neighbors, and strangers. The church is the presence of Christ in the world, the means by which God knits us into community in order to transform our lives and the lives of those around us.

Later, they talked honestly about the great gifts they had received through belonging to a community of faith and from their relationship with Christ. People described how the faith community had helped them rear their children, and they recounted tender moments of grace that had sustained them during seasons of grief. They gave God thanks for close friendships that had shaped their lives and given them insight for dealing with life's challenges. Moreover, the leaders considered honestly, and with humility, what they thought had been the greatest contribution each of them had made to building the body of Christ. Some talked about mentoring students about the faith, others about mission projects they had led, and others about financial gifts they had given. They concluded that the greatest contribution they can make to the body of Christ is to offer love or help a newcomer feel genuinely welcome so that she or he receives what each one of them had received.

The fruit of the learning experience was multiplied as each of those who participated initiated similar conversations in the ministries and groups to which they belonged until the culture of the church started to shift.

Our Actual Neighbors

Many people, despite our prayerful encouragement and invitation, will never visit a church facility or attend a worship service with us. To offer the grace of Christ, we have to do as Jesus did and engage people where they are rather than expecting them to come to us.

Some faith communities have used *The Art of Neighboring: Building Genuine Relationships Right Outside Your Door*, by Jay Pathak and Dave Runyon, to shift the culture toward more outward-focused thinking (Baker Books, 2012). The book uses a diagram and an exercise to deepen our understanding of hospitality with those who live closest to us. The diagram has nine boxes, three across and stacked three high. We're asked to write our home address in the middle box. This box represents where we live, our own home or apartment. The eight empty boxes around it represent the households of the people who live nearest us.

In an exercise I find personally convicting, the book asks us to answer three questions about the people who live in each of those houses represented by those eight boxes.

First, write the names of the people who live in the house represented by the box.

Second, write down some relevant information about the people who live in each of the eight houses, some data or facts that you couldn't learn just by standing in your driveway and looking at their home.

Third, write down something more you know about them because you've shared a conversation or experience with them (paraphrased from *The Art of Neighboring*, p. 37).

Ray Altman, pastor of Leander United Methodist Church in Leander, Texas, preached a sermon series based on the *Art of Neighboring* and led a well-attended discussion group along with it. The conversations helped people see their neighborhoods as places God has sent them, and to view their neighbors as people to intentionally meet and get to know. The focus on neighboring resulted in countless stories of people relating to their neighbors more intentionally and prayerfully, meeting and forming relationships that led to meaningful conversations and connections.

Ben Trammell, pastor of University United Methodist Church, San Antonio, used *The Art of Neighboring* with leadership teams and in a sermon series at churches earlier in his ministry. "Instead of accidents of geography, neighbors become the reason we live where we live," he says. "People made a playful contest out of it. People received points for each box they filled out on the chart as they learned more about the people who lived around them or had a meal with a neighbor. Those already naturally inclined to throw a block party came to see such activities as having a kingdom impact, which led to longer conversations about how the ordinary and everyday part of our life can be the very thing God calls us to use for the cause of Christ."

Even those of us who have learned to love our neighbors through many years of belonging to a church find it difficult to muster the courage to knock on a door of an unknown neighbor and introduce ourselves. It feels risky, awkward, uncomfortable. It's easier to welcome the stranger than to become the stranger. We feel vulnerable. It feels a bit radical! God's grace frequently pushes us to places outside our comfort zone where we would never go if left to our own inclinations. Becoming the stranger in another person's space requires humility.

Some churches have adapted the chart with the nine boxes for use by people sitting in their seats while attending worship, with the boxes referring to people sitting in front of them, beside them, or behind them. Do we know their names, or anything about them? Have we ever shared with them a conversation or experience?

Congregational studies, sermon series, and shared readings help a church learn. These conversations foster a hospitality we carry with us wherever we live and work and play. They teach tangible ways for mission to become a way of life for Christians.

WHO ARE OUR NEIGHBORS?

Many children's sermons include lines like "Are the children of Africa our neighbors?" Everyone shouts, "Yes!" "Are the children of Asia our neighbors?" "Yes!" This rightly fosters a sense of relationship with people everywhere. However, it's easier to love a neighbor in general than a person in particular. Jesus tells the story of a wealthy person who loved God, and even loved his neighbors in general. But he never noticed Lazarus, suffering outside his own front gate (Luke 16:17-31). What if Jesus intended for us to love our actual neighbors, the people who live their lives in the same spaces we do?

Why Do People Need Our Church?

What do people need that churches offer? In *Leading Beyond the Walls* (Abingdon Press, 2002), Adam Hamilton reminds us (p. 21) that every church should be clear about the answers to the questions, "Why do people need Christ? Why do people need the church? And why do people need this particular congregation?" Is it too presumptuous, self-righteous, or arrogant to perceive a responsibility, or even a calling, to connect with others or invite others so that they may receive what we have received?

What do those of us who belong to a community of faith receive that our neighbors need? Theologically, the answer may be "a relationship to God through Jesus Christ." This is too abstract for most, and for many it feels heavy-laden with negative experiences of aggressive evangelistic styles. But the question persists. How do we express with integrity and clarity what we hope others receive by belonging to a faith community?

People need to know God loves them, that they are of value. They want to live a life that matters, and to belong to a community that makes a difference. People need to know that they are not alone; that when they face difficulties, they are surrounded by a community of grace; and that they do not have to figure out entirely for themselves how to cope with family tensions, self-doubts, periods of despair, economic reversal, and the behaviors that hurt themselves or others. People need to know the peace that runs deeper than an absence of conflict, the hope that sustains them even through painful periods of grief, the sense of belonging that blesses them and stretches them and lifts them out of their own preoccupations. People need to learn how to offer and accept forgiveness, how to serve and be served, how to love and be loved. They need relationships that remind them that life is not having something to live on but something to live for, that life comes not from taking for oneself but by giving of oneself. People need a sustaining sense of purpose.

Having said that, the last thing anyone wants is to be told by someone else what they need! Inviting people into Christ does not involve pounding people with "oughts" and "shoulds." Some people recognize a yearning or a curiosity, and they search for meaning, for relationship, and for God. But most people discover their need for God's grace and for the love of Christ through the experience of receiving it. Countless people do not know how hungry they are for genuine community until they experience it, never know they need the connection to God that worship fosters until they regularly practice it, and sense something missing from their lives and don't know what it is until they immerse themselves in service to others. When we connect with people through a Bible study, a Dinner Church, a Christian support group, a prayer ministry, a praise team, a service project, or while serving at a food bank, we put ourselves in the most advantageous place to be shaped by the Spirit of God. By such ministries, the Spirit fills the empty spaces in our lives, and God's initiating grace calls us out of ourselves and into the world of Christ's service. The power of a conversation or an invitation to change a person's life must never be underestimated! Perhaps that is how God changed each one of us.

WHEREVER HE WENT

Whenever Rev. Cornelius Henderson shared a meal with friends in a restaurant, he would say to the server after all the orders were taken, "When you bring the food, we're going to have a moment of prayer. If there's anything you'd like us to pray for, let me know." Almost always, the server would ask for prayers for a child, a friend, or a parent. Most were touched by the offer. Often servers would speak with Rev. Henderson as he was leaving, and ask, "How did you know that I needed prayer?" Rev. Henderson, later Bishop Henderson, didn't wait for people to show up at church in order for him to share the grace of God. He carried it with him wherever he went.

Interlaced by Grace

When I worked in a clergy-training program at a hospital, I was called to the emergency room to support an older man whose wife had been brought to the hospital by ambulance. The couple had started their morning with no idea how events would unfold that day. After shopping, they stopped at a restaurant, and while she was eating, she suffered a heart attack and was rushed to the hospital. Shortly after I arrived in the small consultation room with the husband, a doctor approached him to announce that his wife had died. The doctor handed me an envelope that contained her wedding ring, her necklace, and her eyeglasses to give to him. Needless to say, the man was stunned with grief. After a few minutes together, I offered to call his pastor. He did not have a pastor because they belonged to no faith community. I asked if I could call a relative to take him home, and he told me his family was scattered across the country, living many hundreds of miles away. I asked if I could call a coworker to be with him, and he told me he had retired years before from work in another city. What about a neighbor I could call? He told me that he and his wife didn't know the names of the other residents in the apartment since they'd only lived there three years. I helped him with the paperwork, offered a prayer as I held his hands in mine, handed him the envelope that contained the jewelry and glasses, accompanied him to the exit, and watched him walk away alone to cope with the shocking news of the day and to grasp its meaning for himself all on his own.

Life is not meant to be that way. God intends for people to live their lives interlaced by the grace of God with others, to know the gift and task of community from birth to death, to have the interpretive structures of faith to sustain them through times of joy and periods of desperate agony, to have the perspective of eternity, and to "take hold of the life that really is life" (1 Timothy 6:19).

In most communities, 40 to 60 percent of people have no relationship to a church. A majority of our neighbors on the streets where we live do not know the name of a pastor to call when they face unexpected grief. Most of our coworkers have a few close friends and a circle of acquaintances but do not know the sustaining grace that a faith community offers. Most of the families we sit alongside at our children's soccer tournaments and band concerts, most of the students we meet from the university, and most of the people who repair our cars and serve us in restaurants do not have a community where they learn peace, justice, genuine repentance, forgiveness, love, and unmerited grace. Most of those browsing in the businesses where we shop and sitting behind us at baseball games do not know what it's like to join their voices with others in song and how this lifts the spirit. Most of those who share our benches at bus stops, who sit across from us in waiting rooms, who take their children to the school down the block from us do not have a community that prompts them to serve, to take risks for others, and to practice generosity.

BABY GREETER

A church in South Texas developed a "Baby Greeter" ministry. Each week, a woman would welcome guests with infants to show them the nursery, introduce them to the people who would be caring for their children, teach them the security and paging processes, and tell them which restrooms have changing tables. She showed them the comfortable rocking chairs for parents of infants, the cry room, and the crayons and coloring books for young children. She gave them a copy of the childcare policies. Most important, she learned the name of every baby who came through the door.

"We're such a friendly church. We do fine with hospitality." Sometimes the greatest strength of faith communities is also their greatest weakness. Those who already belong grow to love one another so much that their lives and interests become intertwined. These tight-knit friendships become impenetrable to others, cliquish with a closeness that closes out new people. Those on the inside don't even notice; they feel content because their own needs are met. The church becomes inward-focused, blind to the guests who feel like outsiders, and oblivious to the people who live in the immediate neighborhood.

We offer people a way to connect to that mysteriously sustaining community that finds its purpose in the life, death, and resurrection of Jesus Christ. In the life he lived—the lessons he taught, the people he touched, the healing he offered, the forgiveness he gave, the love he showed, and the sacrifice he made—is the life that really is life.

Hospitality means we pray, plan, prepare, and work toward the purpose of helping others receive what we have received in Christ.

Radical Hospitality?

If the biblical quality of hospitality includes all these things, why intensify it with the word *radical*? What is Radical Hospitality?

Radical describes practices that are rooted in the life of Christ and that radiate into the lives of others. *Radical* means "drastically different from ordinary practice, outside the normal," and so it provokes practices that exceed expectations, that go the second mile, that take welcoming the stranger to surprising new levels. By *radical*, I don't mean wild-eyed, out of control, or in your face. I mean people offering the absolute utmost of themselves, their creativity, their abilities, and their energy to offer the gracious embrace of Christ to others.

Churches characterized by Radical Hospitality are not just friendly and courteous, passively receiving guests warmly. Instead, they exhibit a restlessness, an unsettling awareness of those who stand in need of grace. They are genuinely curious about and interested in forming relationships with people outside the faith community. They are eager to carry Christ's initiating love with them into their daily lives.

Faith communities practicing Radical Hospitality offer a surprising and unexpected quality of depth and authenticity in their caring for the stranger. People intuitively sense that "these people really care about me. They genuinely want the best for me. I'm not just a number, a customer, a target in their strategy to grow their church. I'm welcomed along with them into the body of Christ." This is Radical Hospitality. Such faith communities surprise people with a glimpse of the unmerited gracious love of God that they see in Christ.

Radical Hospitality Changes Everything

Radical Hospitality shapes the work of everyone who offers Christian service and leadership in the faith community. Everyone prays, plans, and works so that their specific ministries with children, missions, the facility, worship, music, outreach, and study are done with excellence and with special attention to newcomers and to reaching out to others wherever they are. *Radical* intensifies expectations and magnifies the central importance of this relational element of our life together in Christ. Radical Hospitality means we offer our utmost and highest, and we do it joyfully and authentically, not grudgingly or superficially, because our initiative represents the initiating love of Christ.

All churches offer some form of hospitality, but Radical Hospitality describes faith communities that exceed expectations. Congregations that practice Radical Hospitality do not settle for mediocrity; they strive for excellence.

Two examples illustrate the difference Radical Hospitality makes: summer programs for children and the leadership team responsible for property and facilities.

Many churches offer vacation Bible school or some other discipleship activity for children during the summer. If we asked some churches, "What's the purpose of this program?" we might receive the answer, "For our children to have a fun experience while school is out." If the purpose of the summer ministry is simply for children to have fun, then why not load them into a van, take them to the movies, and let them spend time with their friends? Such a purpose cannot sustain a children's ministry with integrity.

Other congregations answer, "The purpose is so that *our children and grandchildren* hear about God and learn the stories of the faith through songs, crafts, drama, and other enjoyable activities." The ministry now serves a higher purpose. Clearly stating this purpose guides the leaders in selecting people to serve as teachers, choosing curriculum, and planning communications. If someone brings a friend, leaders view it as an added delight, a good opportunity to warmly welcome a guest. This attitude is basic Christian attractional hospitality.

Now imagine a church that takes this further: "The purpose of our summer children's ministry is so that our children and grandchildren *and the children of the neighborhood* hear about God and learn the stories of the faith so that more families experience Christ's love through a genuine faith community." Radical Hospitality makes an obvious difference. To focus programs, not just on the children of those who already belong but also upon those who have never attended church, guides planners to use other forms of communications about the event—posters in local businesses, flyers on bulletin boards in Laundromats, signs on the church lawn, handouts to parents at a public playground, banners and yard signs in the neighborhood. To be driven by this purpose means that planners might change the location, dates, and times of the children's ministry, perhaps holding activities in a park or cooperating with a neighborhood school close to concentrations of younger families, even if that location is a considerable distance from the church facility. The desire to reach children of families who do not already belong to the congregation might mean that the planners invite leadership differently, particularly choosing teachers and musicians who have a gift for making newcomers feel at home. It might mean offering aspects of the ministry in another language. An outward focus inspires planners to gather information on each child who participates so that leaders can follow up with families. Planners would evaluate success not just by how many of their own children participate in the ministry, but by how many new families the church forms relationships with and how many people move toward greater involvement.

With the Spirit's prompting, there is no end to how far a congregation might go. Some churches offer Sidewalk Sunday school, sending vans full of teachers into neighborhoods full of kids in areas beyond the usual range of the church's outreach, where they provide for an hour of stories, singing, crafts, and teaching close to where the children live and play.

Growing churches say *yes* to ideas that declining churches say *no* to. They are willing to do things other churches are unwilling to try.

Let's look at another example. Most committees tasked with oversight of the church facilities assure that buildings are properly insured, the air-conditioning works, and the roof doesn't leak. In many churches, they simply deal with the crises that arise, and they focus primarily on property, not people. They practice basic hospitality, seeing that people are safe and moderately comfortable while they participate in services and ministries.

Imagine a facilities team that practices Radical Hospitality, viewing their work as a ministry that makes certain that the buildings themselves communicate hospitality, an unmistakable sense of welcome, and complete accessibility: "Our purpose is to ensure that these buildings serve the highest purposes of ministry in Christ's name, and we dedicate ourselves to making the facilities as useful, inviting, friendly, and open as possible."

Such a team continually searches for ways to make the facilities look fresh, appealing, inviting, easy to navigate, safe, clean, and attractive. They don't settle with anything less than the best, and they take immediate action when they notice messy restrooms, peeling paint, musty carpets, inadequate lighting, potholes in parking lots, distracting and inadequate sound systems, or playgrounds overgrown with weeds. People don't allow their houses to fall into disrepair, and they never send their own grandchildren into an unkempt backyard full of unsafe play equipment. Why do they let God's house fall into such disrepair? Facilities speak a message about what the church thinks of itself, how importantly it takes its mission, how confidently it sees its future. Our buildings tell the world what our faith community thinks about children, senior citizens, persons with disabilities, and guests.

Facilities work against our witness if guests struggle to figure out confusing and outdated signs, convoluted hallways, and staircases that insiders have grown accustomed to but which overwhelm newcomers. Radical Hospitality pushes facilities teams beyond discussing merely insurance and leaky roofs.

It is easier to create a culture of hospitality in a physical space that itself communicates welcome.

Most people work in newer buildings with modern lighting, contemporary colors, and fire security systems that make them feel safe. They eat at restaurants and sleep in hotels and attend movies that meet high standards. They are accustomed to quality and cleanliness in restrooms, and they come with high expectations about the safety of the nursery for their children. They feel like they've traveled back in time when they see 1950s institutional green paint, rusty exposed piping and cramped toilets, dim lights in hallways, no windows on the doors of children's classrooms, and no smoke detectors. We can do better.

I visited a church that had changed the time of its worship services and had moved the pastor's office to the former youth room. Two years after these changes, outdoor signs still had the old worship schedule, and the panel on the pastor's office still described it as the youth room. The incident sounds quaint, and members found the delay in updating signs amusing, like a self-deprecating family joke. But they might as well hang a sign that says "For Insiders Only" on the front of the church. Nothing about the facility said, "Welcome. We want you to feel at home here."

Every faith community says that it warmly welcomes people who use wheelchairs or walkers. Our physical spaces speak a different message: "Sure we embrace people with disabilities . . . as long as they can climb up the stairs and slide into the pews just like everyone else!" We can do better.

Radical Hospitality pulls out of us our utmost creativity for the purposes of Christ.

CAFÉ EN LA CALLE

Volunteers from a congregation in Miami arise early on Monday mornings to serve coffee and donuts from a table set up near a street corner where day laborers congregate to connect with people offering short-term jobs. They form relationships, offer prayer, and simply demonstrate the hospitality of Christ. Café en la Calle provides a moment of connection across language, cultural, ethnic, and income divides. The utter simplicity of the ministry replicates the basic connections Jesus asked of his disciples: "I was hungry, and you gave me something to eat, I was thirsty and you gave me something to drink. . . ."

Let's Get Practical

Looking for some simple ways to make guests feel welcome?

o   Update the church website.

o   Seriously. Update the website! And keep it up to date. Without a website, you do not exist to people looking for a church. Nobody can find you. With a poor quality, out-of-date website, what they discover about you does not help.

o   Use social media, Facebook, Instagram, and other means to share video trailers, photos, and information about upcoming events. Tell stories about changed lives.

o   Upgrade the video streaming of worship services. An ever-increasing number of people "attend" online three or more times before showing up in person. It's a low-risk way to see what's going on. Video streaming helps *immobile* members participate (those who cannot get to church any longer) and *mobile* people to stay connected (those who travel frequently).

o   Clean, update, light, or repaint all signage—street signs, entry and welcome signs, and indoor directional signs.

o   Repaint and repair outdoor playground equipment.

o   Teach ushers and greeters to escort people to the place they are asking for rather than merely pointing the way. Make people feel at ease, take note of names, introduce guests to the pastor. Seek to understand the perspective of the newcomer. Anticipate their needs.

o   Welcome everyone of any age, marital status, sexual orientation, income level, ethnicity, or language preference with utmost graciousness. Welcome one another as Christ has welcomed you!

o   Don't pounce on younger guests because of your desperation for young people. Give them space. Don't squeeze them into your mold.

o   Do a nursery makeover. Let young parents make the design and safety choices.

o   Provide free child care at every event, worship service, and church activity.

o Require all persons who serve with young or vulnerable people to be safe sanctuary certified with complete background checks. No exceptions. None. Ever.

o Mark parking spaces for visitors, the handicapped, and parents with infants.

o Remove or shorten a pew or change up the seating in the worship space to make room for wheelchairs (and not just on the last row!).

o Offer a tour of the facilities after services. Talk about ministries and not just buildings.

o Stay available before worship. Foster mixing and mingling. Provide a coffee bar.

o Get the names of guests. Collect contact information in a fun, nonthreatening way.

o Start each service with a warm welcome.

o Offer a monthly lunch with the pastor for people who want to know more about the ministries.

o Remove insider jargon and acronyms from announcements and instructions. Make communications "guest friendly."

o Make Christian invitation and welcome a vital part of the culture, an expectation of everyone and of every small group, music team, and serving ministry. Invest serious time to plan, pray for, invite, and receive newcomers, and to teach people to practice biblical hospitality in their personal lives.

o Don't coast the week after Easter and Christmas. Contact every guest who attended. Thank them for being with you. Plan interesting or provocative ministries or sermon series in the weeks after to attract them back.

o Measure the retention rate of first-time guests. How many return? Twenty percent? Thirty percent? Work to increase the percentage. Notice trends.

o Invite small groups to adopt spaces within the church to offer welcome to guests so that they take ownership of their "mission field." Encourage them to form relationships and invite guests to lunch.

o Form teams to greet everyone each week who sits in a particular section in the sanctuary.

o Contact first-time guests within thirty-six hours by email, phone, or with a gift.

o Ask someone from another congregation that excels in hospitality to speak to your leadership. Send people to visit another church that does well with reaching people who have little or no faith experience. Listen and learn.

o Start a "Reading with the Pastor" book study for the core leadership team. Focus on strategies for reaching people and learn about cultural trends related to faith. Learn about next generations.

o Study the demographics of the neighborhood and compare the age, ethnicity, and income trends for people who participate in your church. Ask, "Why has God placed us here?"

o Become a community meeting place for organizations consistent with your mission.

o Remodel the main entryway to make it open, well lit, warm, appealing, and easy to navigate.

o If yours is a strong, vibrant, growing congregation, start a second site to reach a different area or constituency.

o Give people a way to be hospitable in their daily lives. Bee Creek United Methodist Church (near Austin, Texas) gave rosemary plants in the shape of Christmas trees to everyone in worship with cards that read "God loves you, and so do we." People carried these with them and gave them to people where they worked or shopped or dined.

o Preach a sermon series on Radical Hospitality. Lead discussions on *The Art of Neighboring*. People love to learn. Draw them into the task of discipleship. They may be more eager than you can imagine.

o Offer ministries at unexpected places for unexpecting people—at a bikers weekend, a farmers market, a fishing tournament, the morning after the prom, following football games.

o Encourage people to host a monthly Neighbor Night, inviting people near where they live to a simple dinner in their homes for no other reason other than to form relationships. Any time we practice hospitality we provide a glimpse of the extravagantly hospitable God. Little gestures become a sermon in action, even if we use no faith language explicitly.

o Explore Dinner Church, a model of neighborhood dinners followed by faith conversations and prayer.

o Build anticipation for a special "back to school" focus. Offer prayers of blessing over students' backpacks. Bring teachers forward to pray for them.

o Don't let the fear of failure paralyze you into inaction. Even if only a handful of people gather in Christ's name, a great harvest is promised.

Faith communities that practice Radical Hospitality do not look only at the numbers, corralling people through perfunctory processes to get them to join. Instead, they genuinely engage people, listen to them, and help them feel accepted, respected, connected, needed, involved, and loved. They form relationships. They help newcomers grow into the body of Christ's people.

A Change of Attitudes and Practices

Edwards Deming, the genius of organizational systems, observed that "a system produces what it is designed to produce." In this intentionally redundant statement, he reminds us that a system is aligned to get the results it is getting, and it will not get any other kind of results unless something changes.

How is your faith community doing? Are ministries touching the lives of a growing number of people or engaging fewer people each year? Is the average age trending older or getting younger with the addition of new people? Are ministries increasing or decreasing? What about the number of initiatives to form Christian community in places other than church facilities? If yours is like most congregations, it is declining in numbers, increasing in expenses, and serving an older average age of people with each passing year. Deming would tell us that if the congregation established a task force and asked it to develop a plan that would cause attendance to fall and the median age to increase, they would return with a plan that looks exactly like what the church is doing now! Congregational systems are perfectly aligned to get the results they are getting, and that means uninterrupted decline for most churches.

Something must change. People getting mad and leaving is not the cause of decline. The faithful simply grow old and die, and no one takes their places. People are not entering into the life of faith at a rate that matches or exceeds the number maturing and dying.

Too many churches want more young people as long as they act like old people, more newcomers as long as they act like old-timers, more children as long as they are as quiet as adults, more ethnic families as long as they act like the majority in the congregation. To become a more fruitful congregation requires a change of attitudes, practices, and values.

Little changes have big effects, and change can happen in a hurry. I've known people who have belonged to a community of faith and continued to grow spiritually for decades, and it all started with a single conversation and an invitation. People have begun a lifetime of following Christ and serving others because of how someone treated them when they first visited or because someone cared enough to reach out to them during a time of grief. Attending to the smallest details changes the culture of the church.

One small church painted their nursery, trained their nursery staff, replaced the playground equipment, and by word-of-mouth carried the message of their special care for children, and attendance grew from forty-five to fifty-five. And it all started with a paint job! Another church decided to hold one of their Palm Sunday services in a local park. They rented the dance slab, brought in chairs and balloons and bought hundreds of tickets on the mini-train. Pets were welcomed and everyone was invited. The regular congregation invited their friends and many people just walked up and joined in.

A MINISTRY THAT ROCKS!

A rural congregation in Missouri grew over 150 people in attendance. The secret has been an active hospitality that became contagious throughout the congregation. For instance, when a visiting mom felt self-conscious whenever her baby started to fuss during worship, the pastor met with congregational leaders and they decided that they valued having young people so highly that they had to do something to ease the discomfort. To show support for the young mom, they bought a comfortable, well-padded rocking chair and placed it just behind the last pew of the small sanctuary. Word got around, and soon they needed two more rocking chairs to accommodate parents who found this congregation to be the friendliest around! Rocking chairs for moms, an inviting youth room for young people, a new extension that makes the building handicap accessible—the pastor and the congregation use these to help communicate the priority they place on welcoming more and younger people.

Imagine if every serving ministry, music ministry, Bible study, and support group ministry agreed to prayerfully change one practice to develop relationships with younger adults, to serve them and invite them into service. The facilities team might put diaper changing tables in the restrooms, the music team might prepare a musical for children, an older adult class might pay for child care so young parents can attend Bible study. When every ministry changes a little, the cumulative effect changes the direction of the church.

The willingness to risk something new creates a buzz and a stir in the community that strengthens participation in all other ministries of the church. Word-of-mouth is still the most important form of human communication, and when people talk about the experience they've had of warmth, caring, grace, and love, the work of Christ thrives.

A Single Heart

A faith community changes its culture one person at a time. Radical Hospitality begins with a single heart, a growing openness, a prayerful yearning for the highest good of another person. It starts when one person treats another respectfully and loves the stranger enough to overcome the internal hesitations to form a genuine relationship that reflects the hospitality of Christ.

We tend to avoid personal responsibility for discipleship by redirecting conversations toward programs and strategies. People point to the pastor, the staff, or a leadership team, and say, "If they would only . . ." Or, "What they should do is . . ." People blame and scapegoat and find fault for why ministries don't thrive, and they deny and ignore their own complicity in the stagnation of their churches. Newcomers feel alone and shunned, even in a crowd of friendly people, because everyone believes someone else must be connecting with them. This won't change until each one of us takes responsibility for practicing Radical Hospitality as obedience to Christ. Disciples mature from "they ought" to "I will."

Come and See

An invitation is not complicated. In the first chapter of John's gospel, Jesus's invitation was simple: "Come and see" (John 1:39). His disciples then used the same language to invite others. People don't need to know the answers to all the questions of faith to invite someone. They don't need to exaggerate or persuade or say more than is true. They simply and naturally find their own way of saying to those with whom they share common activities, "Come and see."

MULTIPLE BLESSINGS

A large, growing church celebrated the birth of triplets to a couple in the congregation. LeeAnn, the church secretary, believed that the extraordinarily overwhelming task of parenting triplets deserved the prayerful support of the congregation. How could they best minister to parents of multiple births? She contacted the parents of twins she knew in the congregation and asked for their insight. The staff became aware of two other sets of twins, born to families connected to the church day school. A few weeks later, the congregation launched a support group for parents of multiple births, called Twins and More! The church provided high-quality childcare, invited a family counselor to lead the first gathering, publicized the ministry to the general public, and then let the parents establish their own agenda for discussions and activities. Soon several families with no relationship to a church began to attend and then get involved. Radical Hospitality involves seeing a need and taking the initiative to help.

The people who do this best do not fill their invitations with "oughts and shoulds." They don't make people feel guilty or nag them incessantly. They pray constantly for the wisdom of right timing, and when it feels natural, they tell an acquaintance about a service project they are working on or a music team that's doing something special this weekend, and they say, "We'd love to have you go with us." On Monday mornings when coworkers talk about their weekend activities, they're not afraid to say, "I loved working on the Habitat for Humanity project with my church. My back is killing me, but it meant the world to me to be able to help." They find their own voice and say in their own way, "Come and see."

Or when someone new starts work at the office or someone moves into the neighborhood, in addition to the standard gestures of welcome, say, "And if you're looking for a church, we'd love to have you come with us sometime." At other times, when they know someone faces a difficulty in their marriage or suffers the grief of loss, they're not afraid to say, "Something that helped me was talking to my pastor. I know she'd be willing to talk with you, too. If you want her name or would like for me to call her, I'm happy to help."

People have no reluctance telling others where they get their hair cut, where they get their car fixed, where they like to eat. And yet, concerning the most important relationship Christian disciples have—the one to God through Christ's community—they feel hesitant to speak. They don't want to appear pushy or sound fanatically religious. But think of all that relationship to God means, the perspective of faith, the understandings of life, the relationships formed, the sense of meaning and connection and contribution. Why wouldn't we desire these things for the people we share our lives with?

Think of the people we share activities with—parents of other soccer players, people at work, the neighborhood carpool. Pray, and rehearse, and commit yourself to invite them to participate in a ministry or attend a service. Don't be pushy. Do it with integrity. Do it in your own voice. Be faithful to yourself and to God. Practice Radical Hospitality. Do it for Christ's sake.

Go and Do

Jesus also sends us out in his name. To "go and do" does not have to be difficult. Knocking on the door of a neighbor you don't know to invite them for ice cream in your backyard may seem awkward at first, but it's not a complicated task.

Jesus sent his disciples out "to every town and place where he himself intended to go" (Luke 10:1). Imagine how differently we would behave toward our neighbors and those we regularly encounter through our work, leisure activities, and hobbies if we viewed ourselves as being sent by Christ into these spaces and relationships. The neighborhood where you live, the place where you work, and every place you go is a place where Jesus himself intends to go. He's sending you on his behalf as a disciple, an ambassador, with a message of grace, peace, and reconciliation. The smallest act of everyday discipleship can have a huge impact on the life of another, and on your own. Go, and Do!

CONVERSATION QUESTIONS

How do people hear about your church? In what ways are people encouraged to invite and welcome people? How do people learn to practice hospitality?

Is there a consistent plan for welcoming guests who participate in ministries of the church? How are they invited to further relationship?

Which ministries are the easiest for people to connect with? Why?

What is the one activity you could do, which, if done with excellence and consistency, would have the greatest impact on fostering a culture of Radical Hospitality?

How did you become a part of the congregation to which you belong? Describe the experiences and people who opened the doors for you. What obstacles made it difficult to feel like you belonged?

What is one step you are willing to take to practice Radical Hospitality in your own neighborhood?

What routine activities or normal events can you turn into a means of practicing the hospitality of Christ?

GROUP ACTIVITY

Together with others, walk through your church's physical spaces as if visiting for the first time. Talk about what you see, what you smell, what you hear, what you notice that is welcoming and inviting and helpful, and what you find confusing or uninviting or forbidding. Imagine moving through both the indoor and outdoor spaces from the point of view of a child, a teenager, a mother with a baby, and a person with a disability.

With others from your faith community, walk through the neighborhood that surrounds your church. What is the neighborhood like? Are the people who live nearby known to the congregation? How do you suppose they perceive the church?

Read 2 Corinthians 5:17-21. What is the mission of a Christian disciple according to this passage? How should that mission shape our lives? Pray about how God might be calling you to improve your own personal ministry of hospitality by forming relationships with neighbors you don't know.

Chapter Three

The Practice of Passionate Worship

"You shall love the Lord your God with all your heart, and with all your soul, and with all your strength, and with all your mind; and your neighbor as yourself." (Luke 10:27)

T he website for No Walls Church reads: "We all know someone who is seeking God and community but may not feel comfortable in a traditional church service. We believe in worship without walls—no walls in where we meet, what songs we sing, and how we relate to each other. The messages begin with mercy and grace, and connect to ideas that we are already pursuing. The music may be a familiar gospel tune but could also be ripped from your favorite playlist. All are welcome. Come as you are."

No Walls Church, a ministry of Bee Creek United Methodist Church near Austin, Texas, moves from place to place—a winery and bistro, a crafts market, a renovated old church building that serves as a wedding venue, an icehouse.

Worship at Good Shepherd United Methodist Church in Kansas City has an edgy feel, led by a strong praise band with a penetrating beat. The church experimented with celebrating the Sacrament of Holy Communion at every service. "I thought people would get tired of it," Pastor Mark Sheets says, "but we use various liturgical expressions. Four times a year, we celebrate the Sacrament of Baptism instead of Communion, and everyone remembers his or her baptism. Reclaiming the sacraments has given new life to our worship."

Believers Garden is a weekly special needs worship service for adults with cognitive and developmental challenges, offered by University United Methodist Church in San Antonio. The service offers lively interactive praise and worship with more than one hundred people attending. Volunteers take instruments to residential facilities so that adults watching the livestream service can join in making music. Pastor Ben Trammel says it's the most authentic and meaningful worship experiences anyone can imagine. "There's something powerful about worship where all pretense is peeled away, and people speak and pray and sing who aren't concerned about what others think about them. Everything is from the heart."

In the closing of a church in a nearby community, Valley Praise UMC in the Rio Grande Valley of Texas saw an opportunity to adopt and renovate the facility to be its second campus. Valley Praise ministers in communities that are roughly 80 percent Hispanic, 15 percent Anglo, along with a growing African American and Asian population. The overall composition of the congregation matches those demographics almost exactly. Worship services are conducted in English, and some services are translated into Spanish. In translating services, Lead Pastor Aaron Saenz says, "This allows multiple generations to sit together in church—grandparents who may prefer Spanish and grandchildren who prefer English." Further, Valley Praise is reaching the community and reflecting its diversity by operating in common cultural language.

Gruene United Methodist Church in New Braunfels, Texas, offers worship under a bridge that spans a river in the heart of the city. The bridge provides protection from the elements for homeless people. The service is one of several ministries to serve the homeless.

In St. Louis, BarChurch is part of the vision of The Gathering to create a Christian community that is compelling to new generations. They decided to worship where new generations hang out, at a café bar near the university, because where a Christian community meets is not what makes them a church. Rather, it's what's in the hearts of those who gather.

Leander United Methodist Church uses the homes of their members as spaces of discipleship, community, and mission. Friends and neighbors feel comfortable visiting to eat and chat. The church leverages these comfortable spaces by inviting neighbors to a meal followed by times of prayer and reflection. Home-based faith communities have become authentic places to experience church for those who may never hear a sermon from a pulpit.

A pastor in the Texas Hill Country offers Holy Communion at a table set up at a farmers market.

On Ash Wednesday, a pastor in Missouri puts on her clergy robe and stands on the sidewalk near a university to dispense ashes and offer prayer for anyone who desires it. Another does the same at a feed store along a county highway in Texas.

A young couple who live in a rural neighborhood near Mission, Texas, transforms their small backyard into a place of worship for their neighbors, inviting a lay minister to lead.

On Good Friday in a San Antonio church, the orchestra and choir present a setting of the Requiem, and fourteen hundred people participate.

Look afresh at the worship services your church currently offers. How could we deepen our worship life to make our services more authentic, compelling, and life-changing? It's time to experiment with a greater variety of settings and expressions of worship so that we can form relationships with people who are unlikely to step into a church building. Let's learn to take worship to the places where people naturally gather.

Authentic, Alive, Creative, Life-Changing

Worship as people imagine it is why people don't come to church. People who have little or no experience with churches imagine worship as boring, pious, judgmental, impenetrable, poorly planned, empty of meaningful content, irrelevant, and full of confusing symbols, archaic references, and music from a bygone era. Or they imagine worship as something slick and shiny, a polished performance that is inauthentic showmanship and self-serving.

And yet, people are genuinely searching for a faith community that is authentic, alive, creative. They desire a deeper spiritual life. They are open to experiencing God. People may not want to join a church, but they want to be part of something that matters, something compelling, a faith community that makes a difference in their own lives and lives of others.

Fruitful faith communities practice Passionate Worship. Passionate Worship connects people to God, to one another, and to the world around them. People gather consciously as the body of Christ with eagerness and expectancy; encounter Christ through singing, prayer, scripture, and Holy Communion; and respond by allowing God's Spirit to shape their lives. Lives formed by God's Spirit become the nucleus for faith communities with extraordinary warmth, graciousness, and belonging.

Worship describes those times we gather deliberately seeking to encounter God in Christ. We cultivate our relationship with God and with one another as the people of God. We don't participate in worship to squeeze God into our lives; we seek to meld our lives into God's. Whether we gather in a chapel or in a living room, worship provides a time and place to think less about ourselves and more about faith, less about our personal agendas and more about God's activity and will.

Comprehending the meaning of worship requires looking beyond what *people* do to see with the eyes of faith what God does. God uses worship to transform lives, heal wounded souls, renew hope, shape decisions, provoke change, inspire compassion, bind people to one another, and prepare them to serve their neighbor. Worship sends us into the community more consciously aware and spiritually prepared to represent God's hope and become ambassadors of God's grace.

From the Beginning

From the earliest accounts of faith, people gathered to pray, sing, listen for God's word, and share in a common meal. *Synagogue* means "to bring together," and the Greek word for church, *ekklesia*, means "called out of the world," and refers to the calling of people from their ordinary life to gather together in sacred time and space. Worship breathes life into the community of Christ's followers, forms identity, and provides a place of common learning about faith and for listening to God. People express love for God, and experience God's gracious love offered freely. Worship forms communities, shapes souls, corrects self-interest, and binds people to God, and to their neighbor. God reaches for us through worship conducted in traditional and ancient forms as well as services marked with extraordinary spontaneity in unexpected places. Beautiful sanctuaries, backyard patios, public parks, coffee shops, hospital chapels, under the open sky—in every imaginable setting, people can connect with God through worship.

Where is the most unexpected place you have ever experienced worship with others?

Worship was the reason given for why God liberated the Hebrew people from slavery in Egypt. "Let my people go, so that they may worship me" (Exodus 8:1). Worship defines God's people.

In worship, people practice the highest commandment Jesus taught us: "You shall love the Lord your God with all your heart, and with all your soul, and with all your strength, and with all your mind; and your neighbor as yourself" (Luke 10:27). Worship bends hearts toward God as it stretches hands outward toward others.

Through worship, God pardons sins, restores relationships, and changes lives. Jesus tells the story of the tax collector genuinely and humbly crying to God in the Temple, and says, "I tell you, this man went down to his home justified" (Luke 18:14). Worship is the most likely setting for people to experience the renewed relationship with God that Christians call "justification," in which a person accepts that she or he is pardoned, forgiven, loved, and accepted by God.

Teaching about justification by grace through faith, John Wesley reminded early Methodists of how "the new birth" is God's gift-like work in Christ that is received and accepted when people open their hearts to God. Worship provides an environment for conversion (the return to relationship with God) whether quick, dramatic, and memorable, or marked by gradual shaping and nuanced change over time. God expects lives to change in worship: participants become disciples of Jesus Christ; a crowd of people becomes the body of Christ.

How have you seen a person's life change because of what was experienced in worship?

The psalmist describes an eagerness for relationship with God in worship, "My soul longs, indeed it faints for the courts of the Lord; my heart and my flesh sing for joy to the living God. . . . For a day in your courts is better than a thousand elsewhere" (Psalm 84:2, 10). Through the relationship to God, cultivated in worship, the psalmist goes "from strength to strength" (Psalm 84:7), receiving the encouragement and daily renewal that characterizes life in God. People practice and experience resurrection in worship; every worship experience is a little Easter.

When have you ever longed for worship?

Community worship is the time we spend in God's presence with others. Community worship, in whatever style or context, follows an implicit consensus of structure, words, actions, pace, and movement. But worship also includes private aspects like personal devotions, private prayer, meditation, and study. Community worship and personal devotions reinforce each other, adding richness to the experience of each.

One pastor described his objectives in leading worship. In each service, he seeks to engage the intellect, teaching worshippers something new about the content of the faith. This pastor helps his people understand more about God, Jesus, the stories of scripture, the practice of the faith, and the world around them. Worship changes minds. The pastor also engages the heart, reaching the interior life of worshippers. The intimacy of worship helps people know mercy, grow in hope, sense the Holy Spirit, and offer and receive forgiveness. Worship opens hearts. Finally, the pastor seeks to engage people with a practical challenge to do something differently in their family, community, and world because of their faith in Christ. Worship changes us.

Why Passionate?

Why use *passionate* to describe the practices of fruitful churches?

Without passion, worship becomes dry, routine, boring, and predictable, keeping the form while lacking the spirit. Insufficient planning by leaders, apathy of worshippers, poor quality music, and unkempt facilities contribute to an experience that people approach with a sense of obligation rather than joy. Worship loses its passion. Interpersonal conflict can also threaten the worship life of community, with participants and leaders distracted and exhausted by antagonism. Some services feel inauthentic or self-indulgent as leaders push themselves into the center of attention. Or services can seem as somber as a funeral, when people attend out of obligation, respect, or genuine affection, but privately they wish they were somewhere else. Services sometimes include so many announcements, jokes, digressions, and stories that have nothing to do with the theme, that it feels like a loosely planned, poorly led public meeting. Even with worship in homes, dinner churches, or with online communities, conversation can degenerate into complaining or rumor-mongering. Worship may be the first contact the unchurched have with a faith community, and yet guests may not find genuine warmth or a compelling message. When this happens, people come and go without receiving God.

Worship should express our devotion, our honor and love of God. *Passionate* describes an intense desire, an ardent spirit, strong feelings, and the sense of heightened importance. Passionate speaks of an emotional connection that goes beyond intellectual consent.

Passionate Worship fosters a yearning to authentically honor God with excellence and with an unusual clarity about connecting people to God. Whether fifteen hundred people attend, or fifteen, Passionate Worship is alive, authentic, fresh, and engaging. People are honest before God and open to God's presence, truth, and will. People so desire such worship that they reorder their lives to belong. The empty places in their souls are filled. They experience a compelling sense of belonging to the body of Christ.

In spiritually alive communities, there's a palpable air of expectancy as people gather, a vibrant curiosity about how God's presence will become known. Musicians, readers, greeters, and other hosts arrive early, and with care and eagerness they prepare together, encouraging one another. They genuinely delight in one another's presence, and they give attention to the smallest of details. The gathering, even when it includes many guests, never feels like a crowd of strangers. There's a unifying anticipation, a gracious and welcoming character to the way people speak, act, and prepare. Clearly, the leaders and worshippers expect something significant to take place, and they're eager to be part of it. They expect God to be present and to speak to them a word of forgiveness, hope, or direction. Singing together, joining in prayer, listening to the Word, confessing sins, celebrating the sacraments—through these simple acts, they intermingle their lives with one another and with God. Worship is compelling. It permeates the air.

What creates a sense of expectancy for you as you prepare for worship?

Sometimes we unconsciously enter worship in an evaluative posture as if we were movie critics. We rate the sermon, the time for children, the prayers, and the music according to some internal scale. "How was the service? Well, the sermon was too long, the piano too loud, the children too noisy, and the room too cold." Our attention turns to imperfections, mispronunciations, missed cues, discordant sounds, personal discomforts, the weaknesses of the leaders, and flaws of fellow worshippers.

In a mind-set of expectancy as opposed to critique, worshippers discover that God offers a relationship and seeks to say something through the time together. People are not at worship merely to observe and evaluate but to receive. "What is God saying to me through the words of scripture, even if they are read imperfectly; through the sermon, even if the illustrations are weak; and through the unifying power of music, even if the organist drags the pace? What do we need to hear through the prayer, the creed, and the sacrament? Am I allowing God's Spirit to form me, or am I evaluating the quality of entertainment?"

How do you restrain the evaluative impulse so that you can experience God?

Passionate Worship can be highly formal, with robes, acolytes, stained glass, organ music, orchestral accompaniment, and hardwood pews with hymnals on the rack in front. Or Passionate Worship can take place in an auditorium, gym, public park, or storefront, with casually dressed leaders, videos projected on screens, folding chairs, and the supporting beat of percussion, keyboard, and bass guitar. Authentic, compelling worship derives from the experience of God's presence, the desire of worshippers for God's word, and the changed heart that people deliberately seek when they gather in the presence of other Christians. An hour of Passionate Worship changes all the other hours of the week.

The regular practice of worship gives people an interpretive lens, helping them see the world through God's eyes. Among the many competing interpretive contexts in which people are immersed—fierce individualism, acquisitive consumerism, intense nationalism, political partisanship, hopeless negativism, naïve optimism—worship helps people perceive themselves, their world, their relationships, and their responsibilities in ways that include God's revelation in Christ. The language of the Spirit—love, grace, joy, hope, forgiveness, compassion, justice, community—provides the means to express interior experience and relational aspirations. Stories of faith—scripture, parable, testimony—deepen perception and meaning. The practices of worship—singing, praying, the sacraments—rehearse connection to God and to others. People look at the world in a different way and rehearse their unique calling as people of God and their identity as the body of Christ. Worship changes the way people experience their whole lives.

A Growing Attentiveness

The pastors of a large congregation decided worship had grown routine. Worshippers were not complaining, and attendance was strong. But to the staff, worship had slipped to a lower priority as leaders moved mechanically through their assigned roles. The pastors, music directors, sound and video technicians, secretary, childcare director, and coordinator of ushers planned a day together to focus on the principal worship service. One of the pastors hosted the gathering at her home, and the "mini-retreat" began early in the morning and continued until late afternoon. They evaluated every element of the service and discussed why they do what they do in the way they do it. They considered alternatives and reflected on the theological meanings of their choices. They discussed how each element of worship connects people to God and to one another, and how it could be improved. The gathering, the prelude and the announcements, how and when pastors and choirs enter and exit, and where people stand and how they move—all came under review. They talked about the length, content, purpose, and placement of every action, discussing tone, atmosphere, and pace. Imagining the perspectives of long-term attenders, newcomers, children, and parents with young children, they reviewed lines of sight, eye contact, lighting, sound, visuals. They discussed who led what portions of the service and why, and where worship leaders greeted people before and after the service. They committed themselves to giving more attention to their own spiritual preparation to avoid moving through services by rote.

LITTLE CHURCHES WITHIN A BIG CHURCH

Northern Hills United Methodist Church in San Antonio gives names to their worship services instead of identifying them by meeting times—The Table, The Current, Oasis, La Roca. Some services have their own Facebook pages. Each service is like a little church within the larger church.

These conversations resulted in several changes, some simple and barely noticeable, others affecting texture and tone, and a few altering the service order. They consolidated announcements into one time at the beginning, eliminating the interruptions that broke the prayerful, reflective mood later in the service. They reduced small talk and distracting digressions between elements of the service while maintaining an invitational and gracious quality. They smoothed transitions to improve pace, removing gaps that gave the impression that someone had forgotten what to do. They expanded the pastoral prayer to include more expressions connecting the congregation to the world and they added silent prayer to deepen the sense of unity and awe. They came to consensus about how to use projected images and videos, and limited distracting changes in lighting. Communications problems between musicians and pastors were addressed so that announcements, prelude, and entries flowed more smoothly. Minor seating adjustments removed visually distracting activity behind the preacher during sermons. They agreed upon language to introduce the offering to reinforce the theological underpinnings of tithing, and they developed a consistent way to invite people to Christian discipleship at the close of the service.

The quality, pace, movement, and connection with the people improved. Pastors and staff worked with renewed creativity and purpose. Staff held another mini-retreat to focus on the contemporary service.

More than anything else, the attentiveness to detail and purpose improved the quality of spiritual preparation of the worship leaders. This passion in the leaders shaped how everyone else viewed worship. Worship became compelling again for the leaders, and for the congregation.

How do you spiritually prepare for worship?

For the Love of God

A small congregation approached the renewal of worship differently. The pastor, the volunteer organist, the song leader, and a few regular attenders met to work on how to deepen the worship life of the church. They spent an evening discussing the purpose of worship. They studied scripture, prayed, read a chapter in a book about worship, and concluded that Christian worship is "for the love of God." Then they conscientiously considered what each person might do "for the love of God." They opened themselves to creative change.

One person offered to place fresh-cut flowers in the sanctuary each Sunday, a dramatic improvement over the plastic ones. This she would do "for the love of God." Another said she would arrive early each Sunday "for the love of God" and go through the sanctuary wiping dust from the furnishings, arranging the hymnals, and cleaning up so that the space looked inviting and smelled fresh. The pastor, prompted graciously by the others, decided that "for the love of God" he would work on preaching with a less formal, more relaxed style. He'd make the sermons more practical and useful. "For the love of God" they decided to end each service with

> # WHAT DOES IT HAVE TO DO WITH MY LIFE?
>
> At Leander United Methodist Church, many sermons are followed by a layperson sharing a three- or four-minute reflection, answering the questions "What is the good news? What does it have to do with my life? What am I going to do about it?" The brief talks by someone in the congregation make the sermon more relevant and applicable. About a dozen people take turns offering the reflection. They communicate with the pastor during the week about the content of the sermon. Many times, the after-sermon sharing is deeply moving, connecting the sermon to events going on in the community, the congregation, or their own lives.

everyone holding hands for prayer. They determined to take communion to the elderly and sick who cannot attend, and they would talk to the facilities committee about making the entryway handicap accessible. "For the love of God," the organist even agreed to allow the song leader to sing with recorded music from time to time!

These little changes reveal how much people care about worship, that it matters to them, and that they truly believe something is at stake in this sacred time. Leaders cannot expect other people to take worship seriously if they do not act as if it is important to them.

How Can God Use This?

A congregation that offered a single traditional Sunday morning service with about three hundred in attendance decided to launch a new worship service with the hope of appealing to younger people. They consulted with other pastors who had successfully started similar services, sent people to visit other churches, recruited a music team mostly from among their own congregation, and began coordinating with worship leaders, musicians, and those providing sound, media, and technical support. The pastor, more comfortable with traditional worship, sought coaching from clergy friends. She decided to preach the same content as she did for the traditional service but in a less formal style, using screens and video to reinforce key ideas. A core group of people committed to attend. The service launched in January to take advantage of higher attendance patterns, to benefit from publicity during Christmas services, and to ride momentum of people making New Year's resolutions.

Attendance at the original service remained about the same as before, and attendance at the new service averaged about 135 people. What did the congregation learn through this experience? First, the new service calls forth people and uses their gifts that the original service never did. Musicians who were only nominally active in the faith community before now give hours to the weekly preparation of the service. Second, more middle-aged and older adults attend the service than young people, and young people continue to attend the traditional service in similar numbers as before. Third, the relaxed, informal style requires hard work, good communication, and excellent cooperation to achieve a coherent message. Spontaneity is nurtured with a clear purpose in mind. Fourth, the effectiveness and integrity of the contemporary service derives from the high-quality talent, spiritual maturity, and cooperative disposition of the musicians. Finally, success depends upon the support and encouragement of long-time members, musicians, and leaders who never attend the new service and who have no taste for new worship styles.

Of primary significance is the last point. Key to the success is the verbal support, visible permission, and unequivocal encouragement of leaders and musicians who never attend the new service! Discouragement and conflict result when leaders refuse to give their blessing to creative initiatives. In healthy churches, leaders love people who do not know Jesus more than they cling to their insistence that everyone must worship the same way in the same space. The question "Do you like this?" is replaced by "How can God use this?"

The church that launched the contemporary service realizes that the people who attend the new service look very much like those who attend the traditional service. They have succeeded in increasing attendance among people who already are inclined to visit their church. Their next step is to think about how to offer expressions of worship in places and circumstances where people actually live and work. A spirituality of space—the unarticulated deep feeling that the sanctuary is the only sacred and appropriate place for worship—remains a limiting factor.

John Wesley stretched himself beyond his own traditional tastes and practices and, in his own words, "submitted to be more vile" (*Journal,* April 2, 1739) when he began to preach outdoors in fields to reach those beyond the church's touch. Wesley kept the end in mind—helping people find a way to God and helping God find a way to people—even if it required forms he himself found distasteful. Thank God for his spiritual maturity and liturgical agility! Our rich Christian heritage of worship comes to us through many convolutions of style and practice. Outdoor camp meetings, frontier revivals, high-church liturgies, African American spirituals—these are but a few of many streams of practice that flow through our history.

WORSHIP SHAPED BY THE CONTEXT

When Meri Whitaker was assigned to Canterbury Chapel in the Oklahoma Indian Missionary Conference, the congregation had dwindled to a small group of older, highly committed women. They worked and prayed for some way to reach others with the good news of Christ. Immersing herself in the community, the pastor came to realize the dramatic need for Twelve-Step support groups based on the Alcoholics Anonymous recovery model. The congregation decided to take a risk and adapted their worship to complement and support the twelve steps. Worship became a powerful center for testimony, decision, support, and transformation. Few congregations are as acutely aware of the life-transforming power of worship as Canterbury Chapel.

A hundred years ago, a congregation had three generations present in worship, and all spoke the same language, shared the same culture, grew up with the same stories, and enjoyed the same music. Now congregations include four or more generations, and each has its own way of communicating, its distinctive tastes in music, its own language and culture. If we gather everyone in the same room with so many varying tastes, we cannot assume everyone will stay. But we can open the door to other opportunities for alternative expressions of worship in other settings. Faith communities must be willing to give permission to people to use the music and methods that offer authentic and compelling worship for younger generations. If the people with the greatest influence and resources only support worship that suits their own tastes, the church fails in its mission.

When I visit a church as a bishop, I learn much about the congregation's standard for excellence. If none of the worship leaders know who does what or where to stand and sit; or the communion table is littered with hymnals, a cigarette lighter, a coffee cup and a stack of music sheets; or half the lights above the chancel are burned out; or the choir doesn't know the music, or the microphones whistle and crackle and whine and hiss; or the ushers talk out loud during the service; or the praise team leader introduces a song with an off-color joke; or choir members work crossword puzzles during the sermon; or the pastor insists on telling a self-indulgent and self-congratulatory story before the offering; then what am I to conclude about the congregation's standard of excellence? And what am I to imagine worship is like when the bishop is not present?

Passionate Worship means a church cares enough about the service to offer its best, its utmost every time. People sense deliberate care in preparation and intention. They leave behind grievances, interpersonal rifts, the need for attention, and the desire to control, and they love God with all their heart and soul and strength and mind. By simple acts, lovingly offered, faith communities that practice Passionate Worship draw people to Christ and they afford people the opportunity to be shaped by God.

NO LONGER THE MOST BORING PART OF WORSHIP

When you think of announcements in worship, what comes to mind? Glazed expressions? Last-minute requests? A list so long it hurts?

At Bee Creek United Methodist Church, the morning announcements became a way to meet the people and businesses in the community. The pastor, Laura Heikes, decided to record video announcements. She prepared the simple script and invited a variety of people to read them. It took only minutes to recruit volunteers and to stitch their videos together using a free app on her phone.

The "announcers" may be part of the congregation or not connected to the church at all. One week, the elementary school mascot gave the announcements and all the kids squealed with joy. Another week it was the firefighters at the local station. Fitness instructors, bankers, and baristas have been on the church's video screens. Sometimes Laura links the topic with the announcer, like a teacher inviting the congregation to load backpacks for school kids, or a dentist telling the congregation about how the church is providing critical dental care to those in need in the community. Announcements, once a boring monologue, have become an invitation to see the larger community.

The congregation rings with laughter and true joy when the announcements begin. There are no more last-minute add-ons that stretch out the time because the videos are filmed in advance. The church is getting to know their neighbors through asking people to read announcements and the community is getting to know the congregation.

The Heartbeat of Life

Worshipping God is the heartbeat of life in faith communities.

Worship leaders plan extensively. They talk together, pray together, and walk through every element of the service together. Liturgists prepare their readings, musicians rehearse their specials, technicians review slides and videos. They love worship and long to offer their best to the glory of God.

Looking for ways to improve the worship life of your community of faith? Let's start with the obvious:

- o Always assume visitors are present.
- o Provide excellent, safe, reliable, trained childcare for all services.
- o Serve coffee in several places before and after services.
- o Update the sound system so that it is trouble-free and crystal clear.
- o Make the worship order user-friendly, attractive. and easy to follow.
- o Keep the worship area clean, inviting, fresh, and attractive.
- o Make friends with multimedia. Strive for excellence, attend workshops, engage with friends, practice. Integrate visual media so that it's seamless, helpful, and never distracting.
- o Use children's art for slide images or bulletin covers.
- o Have crayons, coloring books, and puzzles for children to take with them into worship.
- o During prayers or as people gather, project a photo or video of the sun rising, of rain falling, or scenes from the community captured by mobile phone during the previous week.
- o Invite students to plan and lead worship.
- o Update lighting, video, and sound systems.
- o Provide comfortable chairs with arms for older adults or people with limited mobility.
- o Provide large-print bulletins.

o   Create children's time that actually speaks to the children.

o   Practice the sermon privately or with someone to give feedback. Engage a speech teacher.

o   Assure that the music is at least good, usually excellent, but never mediocre. Music speaks directly to the soul, setting the tone and the emotional texture of the service. Music may be simple, but it must be dynamic, inspirational, and high quality. Singing unifies people, strengthens the sense of belonging, provokes reflection, and lifts the spirit.

o   Place special emphasis on services for back-to-school, Christmas Eve, New Year, and Easter Sunday services, knowing the disproportionate opportunities these services offer for worship to touch the lives of people from all parts of their community.

o   Share everything you learn. Attend worship and music workshops. Visit other churches. Gather worship leaders from three or four churches, and share ideas. Search the internet for helpful resources. Worship that is alive and compelling requires cultivation to keep it fresh.

More specifically, go deeper in plans to improve worship services.

o   Adopt or create a common daily devotional guide for every household at least once a year that focuses on a particular sermon series or liturgical season.

o   Hold twenty-four-hour prayer vigils for focused prayer for important events.

o   Prepare high-quality, widely communicated special services, studies, musicals, concerts, or children's ministries during Advent, Lent, and Holy Week.

o   Prepare and publicize at least two or three sermon series a year with interesting or provocative themes that draw people into a several-week period of renewal, study, and reflection.

o Hold a music camp for children, with activities to learn about worship through music and drama.

o Nurture your personal spiritual life. Authenticity and integrity derive from the personal practice of faith.

o Demonstrate adaptability, a willingness to learn new ways to serve people. Don't become stuck, resistant, or rigid, and insist only on your own way.

o Make worship an essential element of every mission initiative, student program, adult retreat, financial campaign, and discipleship group.

o Immerse every ministry in prayer.

o Develop disciples who feel competent and comfortable in leading prayers for choirs, classes, kitchen crews, work teams, and hospital visits.

o Invite people to write devotions for Advent, Lent, the newsletter, the website, or special programs.

o Teach people to pray, offer classes, studies, and retreats. Provide quality resources for private devotions. Pray without ceasing.

Congregations that practice Passionate Worship experience the sacraments of Holy Baptism and Holy Communion as a means of grace, ways by which God actively forms disciples and builds the body of Christ. They view infant baptism as initiation into the body of Christ, an expression of the unmerited gracious initiative of God's love. They instruct parents with care, assist the whole church in understanding the significance of baptism, and take time to make the symbols come alive for people of all ages.

Leaders use the Communion liturgy to engage people with the words, the story, and the symbols through inflection, pause, emphasis, voice, tone, and movement. They feel confident and familiar with the liturgy and respect the mystery of the sacrament while making it appealing and accessible. They do not lead Communion spiritually unprepared, and they administer the sacrament in a personal manner, never mechanical, with graciousness and humility.

Leaders who practice Passionate Worship strive for an open quality to every service, making it easy for people to participate and connect. They invite people to take the next steps in their spiritual journey. Everything says, "We're glad you're here. Come back. Learn more. We'll help."

Such leaders give worshippers multifaceted pathways to the truth of Christ. They use a mixture of complex and simple elements, a rhythm ranging from fast-paced and upbeat to reflective and quiet, and a tone that varies from winsome to respectful. Variation speaks both to heart and mind, and addresses those who prefer linear verbal progression as well as others who learn through images, metaphors, and stories. They address more than one or two of the five senses. Silence as well as song deepens unity. Visual focal points draw people's attention toward a cross or communion table. The bread tastes good and smells freshly baked, flowers are fresh, and candles glow with real flames. In traditional sanctuaries, stained glass retells the stories of faith and the building's architecture lifts the eyes and heart. In contemporary settings, well-lit screens show images carefully selected to supplement the purpose of the service and not to detract from it. Everything supports the message. Worship is approachable, accessible, and comprehensible.

Two Approaches

Deepening the worship life of a community involves interweaving two approaches into the planning at once: enhancing the quality of existing services and multiplying the opportunities and settings for worship. Leaders must work both on how to do things better, and how to do different things. Focus on ideas for multiplying opportunities and doing things differently:

o   Offer the Sacrament of Holy Communion in unexpected places.

o   Worship in a prison or juvenile detention center, complete with excellent music.

o   Experiment with Dinner Church.

o   Hold Palm Sunday services in a public park.

o   Start a Twelve-Step Recovery service.

o   Launch an alternative worship service that reaches a different range of interests through different musical styles, or even in a different language.

o   Livestream services. Engage with people who participate in the services, and form online conversations.

o   Develop a YouTube Channel with your church's services and music.

o   Worship at a refugee center.

o   Form relationships with people in a particular community—in an apartment complex, a trailer park, a neighborhood, a favorite restaurant. Share meals. Become a newcomer and welcome the newcomer. Earn the trust to begin conversations about faith and life. Pray together. Experiment with simple forms of worship. Take worship to where people already gather.

Imagine

"I am the vine," Jesus said, and "you are the branches" (John 15:5). Worship connects the branches to the vine, keeps people connected to the source of life, and helps them grow in Christ. Worshippers who are absent feel that they have missed something, and they also feel missed. There's a contagious quality to authentic, compelling worship. Just as in the early church, God adds to their number day by day because worshippers naturally invite those with whom they have other things in common, bearing witness to the spiritual sustenance they've found. Worship nourishes all other ministries, giving life, direction, and encouragement to the whole body of Christ.

Everyone has a role in fostering Passionate Worship.

Imagine a faith community asking each ministry, class, study group, fellowship, choir, band, mission team, member, guest, and volunteer to do something extra "for the love of God" to strengthen community worship.

Imagine leaders reviewing the functionality and effectiveness of microphones, sound systems, and lighting, and looking through the chancel, sanctuary, foyer, and nursery to see that these places look fresh, inviting, clean, safe, and well-lit.

Imagine a congregation-wide prayer ministry. The congregation might print seasonal devotional collections, soliciting volunteers to compose meditations, and distributing them so that everyone is reading and praying the same material at the same time.

Imagine women planning an overnight Lenten or Advent retreat at a hotel, guest house, or retreat center to focus on prayer or other spiritual disciplines.

Imagine people stepping forward to serve by using their technical experience to establish an excellent website, livestream capacities, email newsletters that follow up with thoughts on the previous week's sermon and preparation guides for the week to come.

Imagine laity assuring that the pastor and staff have adequate time every week for spiritual preparation and worship planning. Imagine the faith community funds travel to workshops and seminars on worship and preaching.

Imagine ushers, greeters, nursery personnel, and other hosts meeting to pray and discuss how to deepen the hospitality so that it exceeds all expectations.

Perhaps no one effort would improve worship by 100 percent. But maybe a hundred things would improve by 1 percent, and the passionate love of God evidenced in these changes would renew congregational life.

Jesus mostly taught outside the synagogue and temple. He used spaces like hills and homes and shoresides. He found teaching opportunities in ordinary things like flowers, birds, and fields. He used simple examples drawn from people's everyday lives.

Imagine your congregation boldly taking worship to other spaces. Church on a Trail is an outdoor worship experience of Berkeley United Methodist Church in Austin, Texas. People meet in the parking lot of a nature area once a month before hiking into the woods to sing and share words of grace and encouragement before a time of prayer and contemplation. People stay for snacks and conversation, and return at their own pace, pondering a question given them by the pastor, Wilson Pruitt. The gathering reaches beyond the congregation by posting invitations on various hiking sites, and they use the Meetup social network to stay connected. Imagine the laity who could offer similar patterns of worship among people who share their hobbies and passions.

The responsibility for the quality of spiritual life in the congregation does not reside only with the pastor. Staff can't do it on their own. What each person brings to worship shapes the experience for everyone. Passionate Worship begins with each individual.

One way to deepen the experience of worship is for each person to spiritually prepare before attending. Nothing reinforces the practice of community worship better than a vibrant personal devotional life. Many churches share scriptures and sermon topics on social media during the week so that people can prepare for worship. Other churches encourage people to take notes, or they provide a sermon outline so that people can rethink the key points at home after services.

Worship soars on the God-given gifts of people. All individuals must offer their best as they sing and serve to support authentic, excellent worship.

John Wesley, in his 1761 "Directions for Singing," encouraged early Methodists to "sing lustily and with good courage. Be aware of singing as if you are half dead or half asleep, but lift your voice in strength. . . . Above all, sing spiritually. Have an eye to God in every word you sing. Aim at pleasing him more than yourself, or any other creature."

In how we sing and pray, in how we greet others, in how we approach the sacraments, Passionate Worship reveals our love for God, our desire to open ourselves to God's grace, and our eagerness for relationship to God.

People come to worship carrying many concerns. Some worry about a cousin serving in the military; others face financial struggles that tear at the fabric of family life. Some sense a disturbing lack of fulfillment in their careers, fear health challenges, or feel deeply affected by the immensity of a distant tragedy. Some face monumental decisions while others must constantly moderate conflict at home. Some are overwhelmed with gratitude, humbled by feelings of love, or seeking discernment before a major decision.

Every congregation, large and small, is a tapestry of hope and hurt, a collage of experience and anticipation, a patchwork quilt of gifts, needs, fears, and aspirations. People come to connect to God and one another as well as to feel restored, reminded, remembered, and refreshed. They wonder what God has to do with all that's going on inside of them and in the world around them. Having a relationship with Christ changes their lives. In their searching, God finds them, heals them, sustains them, and forms them anew.

The motivation for enhancing the quality of worship and multiplying the opportunities for worship is about allowing God to use us and our congregations to offer a more abundant life for all. God works through us to change the world. Worship is God's gift and task, a sacred trust that requires our utmost and highest.

The spiritual life depends on more than what happens during a weekly period of worship. This leads us to the next practice of fruitful congregations: Intentional Faith Development.

CONVERSATION QUESTIONS

How does the congregation encourage the pastor, staff, laity, and musicians who lead worship to give adequate time to the preparation of worship?

How are children made to feel welcome in worship? How do young people learn to pray?

What practices, readings, resources, or relationships sustain your own personal devotional life?

The No Walls Church story that begins this chapter says, "We all know someone who is seeking God and community but may not feel comfortable in a traditional church service." Who does this bring to mind for you? What alternative expressions of worship can you imagine your church offering?

GROUP ACTIVITY

Arrange for several of your class members who have never done so to sit in the chancel or choir loft during an entire worship service. Then ask them about what they noticed or learned about the practice of worship or about the congregation as it worships. How does sitting up front change their perception of worship?

Chapter Four

The Practice of Intentional Faith Development

They devoted themselves to the apostles' teaching and fellowship, to the breaking of bread and the prayers. (Acts 2:42)

In a remote village a half-day's walk outside of Jerusalem, a woman fed dried branches into a fire as she prepared to make bread for the day. She dipped her hands into the water of a small basin that sat beside the vase she had carried from the well before sunrise. She sighed deeply at the prospect of another day of unending work just to scrape enough food together to feed her daughters and herself. Since her husband's sudden illness and death, she had felt abandoned and alone in ways she could barely fathom. As she felt the cool water trickle through her fingers, she thought about the story she had heard the night before as she gathered with her neighbors for prayer and supper. It was a story about a woman who met Jesus at a well, where he talked about "living water." She also remembered the story someone told about Jesus touching the man who had been paralyzed for so long. Then a stream of stories cascaded through her mind, tumbling one into another. She thought about a shepherd and his sheep and a woman and her coin, two women's tears of sorrow and joy before an empty tomb, and a poor widow giving more than all the rich people in the Temple. She smiled to herself thinking about that last one.

She had heard about Jesus for the first time only a few months earlier, and now his stories were hers. Word spread about his horrible death (Jesus had been only a couple of years older than her husband when he had died), and then, amazingly, about his being alive and about his followers gathering first in Jerusalem and then here and there in other villages. There were stories of Jesus spoken in the Temple that were retold in the streets and talked about in the homes among her friends. She began to listen, and what she heard amazed her. And the people who told the stories invited her into their homes. She could hardly believe their invitation. Everyone knew that without a husband, she was on her own, destitute. But these people treated her differently. She and her daughters ate with them, receiving more than they could ever repay. And they prayed for her and with her for her daughters. This unexpected love changed everything in her life. Suddenly, she didn't feel abandoned and alone; she felt connected and loved, like her life counted for something. Then she couldn't get enough of the stories or of her friends, these followers of Jesus. Whenever and wherever friends gathered to retell the stories, she was there, and she then retold them to her daughters and other neighbors. She loved learning more about Jesus, hearing about God, and building friendships with others. The stories carried her to the well and back each morning and sustained her through the daily task of feeding her family; and with the stories in her heart and friends at her side, the burdens felt lighter and the days more full of life.

Seventeen hundred fifty years later, in a small thatched-roof cottage in a village an hour's ride from London, a man held his small journal closer to the lamp as he wrote his account of the evening's gathering. It had been a long day. He began working the fields before sunrise and labored alongside other men from the village until after sunset. But unlike many of the others, his day did not end with his work in the field. Instead, he washed up as best he could and ate a quick meal so that he could prepare his home, reread the scripture quietly to himself, and pray for the Spirit's guidance. As Methodist Class Leader, he prayed for each person he expected to come before they arrived. One by one they began showing up until his home was filled with the welcome and laughter, the blessings and good-natured chatter of a dozen of his friends and brothers. Their congenial and affectionate greetings brought warmth beyond what his small hearth could provide. These men had also spent the day laboring, some in stables and fields and others in shops and kitchens.

When everyone had arrived, he reminded them of Mr. Wesley's rules for classes and about the covenant they had made with one another in order to belong: to attend the public worship of God, including the reading and expounding of the Holy Scriptures and receiving the Supper of the Lord, and to commit to private prayer and the studying of scriptures. Leaning toward the lamp, he read to them of their pledge to watch over the souls of one another, to practice diligence and frugality, to do good in every way, and to be merciful as far as possible to all people. Then he led them in singing and prayer, and began to describe how he had experienced the week, joys and sorrows, temptations and trials, and times when God had delivered him. He asked the others about the state of their souls, and each in turn spoke of his life and God's grace during the week past. He shared the scripture that he had prepared, and talked about the thoughts that had come to him about these verses while he had worked the fields during the day. He led them in praying for one another and then collected coins from each to give to the steward for the work of God, carefully recording the amount beside the name of each giver. He offered the blessing of Christ, and they bade him warm farewells to return to their own homes, leaving him with his journal. He noted attendance and marked his appraisal of the spiritual state of each member. Then he snuffed the lamp and took his rest. It had been a long day, but he felt grateful beyond words for his life, his faith, and his friends. He felt renewed, strengthened, and encouraged. By his work in the fields, he made a living. By his care of souls, he made a life.

Two hundred fifty years later, in community you might recognize, a young woman pulls into the church parking lot just before the session begins. She's running a little late. Like most Tuesdays, she's still wearing her suit from work, her evening a blur of movement from office to school to soccer practice to drive-thru to church. Her son dumps his fast-food wrappings in the trash bin beside the door as he carries his schoolbooks into the building. He'll work on homework while Mom does her "Bible thing." She slips into the room as the video begins. Her closest friend is there and welcomes her into the seat beside her. They had signed up for this together, deciding to "just do it" after years of wanting to study the Bible. The class also includes two couples, two older women, a graduate student from the university, and the leader, recently retired from the bank. She didn't know most of these people before they signed up for Bible study, but she's been amazed at how much she's learned from them as they've shared their thoughts about faith and God and scripture and about how much she's come to care for them as they've shared their lives. Tuesday evening has become a time of refreshment for her each week, an oasis of encouragement, learning, and support. For ten minutes, they listen to a video about the stories of Moses, his birth and marriage and encounter with God. Then they walk through the readings, sharing observations and questions.

Every day for the past week, she has spent time reading scripture, sometimes lost in the archaic customs and confused by the stories and characters. She has so many questions about God. She wasn't sure she had time for this kind of study, and sometimes even now she thinks she's wasting her time. Moses seems way back then and way over there. Then the leader talks about Moses's call—the bush, the fear and humility, and the excuses and justifications given to avoid doing what God asks. Her stomach tightens as she hears people tell about times they've felt called by God to do something and have repeated the same excuses themselves. She looks at her own notes from her reading through the week, and sees the questions she wrote. "How does God call people? Sometimes I feel called, but I've never heard voices or seen burning bushes. Is God calling me?" She shares her questions with others and discovers that they wrestle with the same thoughts. The evening ends with prayer, and after she drives home with her son, sends him to bed, and nestles herself into her favorite chair, she finds herself praying, asking, and hoping, "What would you have me do, Lord?"

Perfecting Us in the Practice of Love

Vibrant, fruitful, growing congregations practice Intentional Faith Development. From the first generation of Christians to the youngest generations of faithful people today, the followers of Jesus mature in faith by learning together in community, often with people whose life experiences are very different from their own. Faith communities that practice Intentional Faith Development offer a variety of high-quality learning experiences that help people understand scripture, faith, and life in the supportive nurture of caring relationships. Classes, Bible studies, short-term topical studies, children's church, camps, retreats, support groups that apply faith to particular life challenges, dinner conversation gatherings, and youth ministries are only a few of the countless ways by which congregations help people probe God's will for their lives and for the world, and bring people together to strengthen the body of Christ by building friendships and relationships. Christian disciples strive to develop faith and grow in Christ-likeness through study and learning, and God is best able to form disciples when people do this together.

Christ's gracious invitation through Radical Hospitality embraces us and nudges us to open ourselves to forming relationships, and God's transforming presence in Passionate Worship opens our hearts to Christ's pardon, love, and grace, creating in us a desire to follow. Growing in Christ requires more than weekly worship though, and it is through Intentional Faith Development that God's Spirit works in us, perfecting us in the practice of love as we grow in the knowledge and love of God.

Learning in community replicates the way Jesus deliberately taught his disciples. His followers grew in their understanding of God and matured in their awareness of God's will for their lives as they listened to Jesus's stories, instructions, and lessons while gathering around dinner tables, on hillsides, and at the Temple. Jesus taught us to learn our faith this way.

Jesus also taught us to learn our faith with people whose life experience is different from our own. The disciples listened to Jesus's stories alongside people whom they would otherwise never meet, some from the "wrong" side of life. They bumped elbows at those dinner tables with people who were scorned, looked down upon and even hated. The disciples were themselves a mixed bag. Jesus did not segregate people or categorize them. He did not group people by type, so that they would experience and grow in faith solely with people they already knew and felt comfortable with. Instead, he demonstrated that we often learn most deeply when we experience community with people whose lives are different from ours.

Following the formation of the church by the Holy Spirit at Pentecost, the earliest communities of Christians thrived as "they devoted themselves to the apostles' teaching and fellowship, to the breaking of bread and the prayers" (Acts 2:42). Notice the dual reference to learning and community.

Paul sprinkles his instructions to the followers of Christ with encouragements to learn, grow, teach, and mature. He presents faith not as something static, a possession, or an all-or-nothing proposition, but rather as something we grow into and strive toward, a putting away of one's "former way of life, [the] old self" to clothe oneself "with the new self" (Ephesians 4:22, 24). We seek to have in us the mind that was in Christ Jesus, allowing God's Spirit to shape our thoughts, attitudes, values, and behaviors. Growing in Christ-likeness is the goal of the life of faith.

The change God works in us through the Spirit results in a deeper awareness of God's presence and will, and an increasing desire to serve God and neighbor. By God's grace, we become new persons. "So if anyone is in Christ, there is a new creation: everything old has passed away; see, everything has become new!" (2 Corinthians 5:17).

This growth in Christ spans a lifetime. Paul writes, "Not that I have already obtained this or have already reached the goal; but I press on to make it my own, because Christ Jesus has made me his own. . . . Straining forward to what lies ahead, I press on toward the goal" (Philippians 3:12-14). Faith moves, grows, changes, matures.

As we mature in Christ, God cultivates in us the fruit of the spirit: "love, joy, peace, patience, kindness, generosity, faithfulness, gentleness, and self-control" (Galatians 5:22-23). These are the qualities to which the Christian disciple aspires.

These interior spiritual qualities are radically relational, and we only learn them in the presence of others through the practice of love. They are refined in community, and not just by reading books and studying scripture. They become real in our lives in the love we give and receive from others and in the things we learn and teach with others. Jesus said, "Where two or three are gathered in my name, I am there among them" (Matthew 18:20). Jesus taught in community so that we would learn to discover his presence in others.

As John Wesley and the early Methodists realized, growth in faith does not come easily or automatically, but requires placing ourselves in community to learn the faith with others. Wesley commended the practices of public and family prayers, the searching of scriptures, the receiving of Holy Communion, and the practice of works of mercy—all in supportive community. We learn the life of Christ and will of God by studying God's Word and through experience with other people of faith. The early Methodist Class meetings, like modern-day study groups and mentoring ministries, provided the means to help people remain faithful in their journey toward Christ. By becoming part of a learning, listening, serving community, we place ourselves in the circumstances that are most advantageous for growth in faith. Bible study and faith sharing are not just about self-improvement but about setting ourselves where God can shape us, intentionally opening ourselves to God's Word and call. God uses relationships to change us.

When has God used a small community of Christians studying and praying together to encourage you?

When we study and learn with new Christians, people who are just beginning to be curious about the faith, or people whose faith experience is different from our own, we grow in especially remarkable ways. In these conversations we can lay aside our own assumptions and start from scratch, examining and testing our spirituality, rearticulating and clarifying our core beliefs. When we listen to the story of someone whose life is different from our own, and hear that person's questions and longings, we can see how we are connected to that person. We develop empathy. We deepen our sense of awe. We glimpse another's wrestling with God and see God revealed even in circumstances that seem strange to us. We understand more about the richness and depth of God's love, grace, and mercy. Our Christian faith is shaped and formed when we study it with close friends and people whose lives are like ours. It is an even more transformative experience to explore the spiritual life with people whose lives are unlike our own.

BIBLE STUDY MESSES WITH YOUR LIFE

Carol joined a congregation, attended worship, and served with various week-to-week projects. One turning point in Carol's faith journey was serving with a Volunteers-in-Mission work project overseas. Then she joined an in-depth Bible study. In the small, supportive community of her class, she encountered truths and insights she had been searching for. More than that, she found God calling her to radically change the direction and priorities of her life. She eventually offered herself to full-time Christian service, changed jobs, and now works as mission coordinator, focused on international ministries. "Bible study messes with your life!" is her good-humored but serious way of telling others about her faith journey. Learning in community helps people explore possibilities that God may have for them that they never would have considered on their own.

The practice of learning in community gives disciples a network of support, encouragement, and direction as we seek to grow in Christ. As we consciously appropriate the stories of faith with others, we discover that our questions, doubts, temptations, and missteps are not unusual but are part of the journey. We are emboldened to new ways of thinking about God and of exercising our faith in daily life. Other people help us interpret God's Word for our lives, offering an antidote to inordinately self-referential or narcissistic interpretations that merely confirm our current lifestyles, attitudes, and behaviors. The fruit of the spirit that we see in Christ (Galatians 5:22-23) cannot be learned apart from a network of relationships. In the intimacy of small groups, we learn not only from writers and thinkers and people of the past through scripture and books but also from mentors and models and fellow travelers in our congregation and outside of it. We give and receive the care of Christ by praying for one another, supporting one another through periods of grief and difficulty, and celebrating one another's joys and hopes. Study groups, fellowship gatherings, service teams, musical groups, and other small faith-forming communities are places for us to learn to "rejoice with those who rejoice," and "weep with those who weep" (Romans 12:15). The sanctifying grace of God bears the human face of our fellow disciples.

We learn and grow in Christ-likeness as we begin to see others as our true brothers and sisters. We notice how God is at work in places and people beyond our own experience, and this inspires, motivates, and strengthens our faith, propelling us to learn and grow in still more new ways.

In addition, learning in community provides accountability for our faith journeys. A seminary professor used to say, "Everybody wants to want to study the Bible." He was referring to the contrast between our good intentions and our actual practices. How many people each year resolve to read the Bible, start with Genesis in January, and give up all hope of seeing their way through to the end by the time they reach Leviticus in February?

I've completed eight marathons, and people often ask me how to get started on a running program. When I ask them what they've tried, they inevitably tell a story about New Year's resolutions and their enthusiastic jump out of bed when the alarm rings at six on the first morning. The eagerness lasts a few days, and during the second week when the alarm screams them awake, they tell themselves, "There's nothing wrong with running at seven rather than six," and so they sleep another hour. By the third week, when the alarm rings at seven, they tell themselves, "There's no sense being fanatical about this; I don't have to run every day to be fit." Then the downward slide begins, from five times weekly to once a week, from two miles to one, from running to walking to nothing at all. That's the course of many good intentions.

Technology companies tap into this human phenomenon in all sorts of ways and offer products to create accountability for people who are striving to achieve fitness, diet, or mindfulness goals. Wearable technology buzzes on our wrists when we've been sitting for too long. Colorful banners appear on our devices reminding us to log our last meal, or drink a glass of water, or hop on the scale. Many of us track our steps each day, with rising anxiety when the hours wear on, but our numbers do not keep up. Community is nearly always a part of these programs, to deepen the sense of accountability. Employees compete on teams to get the most steps and win awards for their efforts. Exercise and diet apps create user networks, so that people can share information, tips, and encouragement with others on the app. Internet exercise programs offer daily workouts and yoga sessions, with live participants in a studio location and virtual participants scattered around the globe, all connecting via their digital devices, using comments and other social media, experiencing a gigantic global real-time workout class.

The answer in physical wellness, as well as in Bible study, is to covenant with people who share the same goals. If we know that people are gathering, leaving a spot for us at the coffee shop or around their dinner table, we'll do what it takes to get there even when we don't feel like it. In community there is a natural accountability. Covenanting together keeps us strong in our convictions and habits. That's why Jesus sent the disciples out two by two to go "to every town and place where he himself intended to go" (Luke 10:1). In pairs, the disciples could build each other up for the task; pray for each other; and support each other through the inevitable resistances, difficulties, misjudgments, and false starts. We learn in community because others keep us faithful to the task of growth in Christ. That's why John Wesley organized the early Methodists into classes, bands, and societies, and that's why churches offer study groups, Bible courses, home dinner conversations, mentoring ministries, other types of classes, and fellowship experiences in the church, in the neighborhood, in the park, and wherever two or three gather in Christ's name. The practices of faith are too demanding without support from others. Other Christians help us pray, read scripture, exercise love and forgiveness, and explore and respond to the will of God for our lives.

One person new to faith struggled to study the Bible even with the plans on his mobile phone Bible app. Then he decided to make his plan "public," that is, let other users, his friends at church, his family, see his progress. He said that after that, not only did he never miss a step, but his sister got more regular in her study because she saw her brother's progress. A friend also reported being more inspired. He was amazed—accountability and inspiring others all because they are using an app that lets you share your progress in a Bible study, highlight scriptures that speak to you, share notes about your own reflections.

Dietrich Bonhoeffer reminds us that an incomparable joy results from the physical presence of other Christians. We see "in the companionship of a fellow Christian a physical sign of the gracious presence of Christ." In community, the Christian no longer seeks "his justification in himself, but in Jesus Christ alone." According to Bonhoeffer, every Christian needs another Christian when she or he becomes uncertain and discouraged. The Christ in one's own heart is weaker than the Christ in the word of a brother or sister (*Life Together*, Harper & Row, 1954, p. 20).

Intentional

This all underscores the importance of faith development. Why add the adjective *intentional* to describe the practice for fruitful congregations? *Intentional* refers to deliberate effort, purposeful action toward an end, and high prioritization. It highlights the significance of faith development and contrasts those faith communities that take it seriously with those that offer it haphazardly and inconsistently, without new initiative, plan, or purpose.

Intentional Faith Development describes the practice of congregations that view the ministries of Christian education, small-group work, faith-forming relationships, and Bible study as absolutely critical to their mission, and so they consistently offer opportunities for people of all ages, interests, and faith experiences to learn in community. They offer opportunities for people to engage in faith development at the church (Come and See), but they also look for ways to offer opportunities for people who may never enter the church or become part of the congregation (Go and Do). They consciously and deliberately cover the whole age spectrum, fostering faith development outside of worship during the course of the year for children, youth, young adults, singles, couples, middle-aged adults, and older adults. They study and analyze the demographic makeup of people in their community, noting people's shared interests, anxieties, and lifestyles, and create ways to meet people wherever they are, spiritually and in everyday life. They actively seek ways to develop opportunities for study, discussion, and growth with and for people outside the congregation—in coffee shops, fitness centers, sports gatherings, public parks, and wherever people gather. They examine their efforts to offer radical hospitality and passionate worship in the wider community, and find ways to create all sorts of small communities for fellowship and study. They host topical discussion nights at the church or a location in the community. They hold ask-a-pastor events, where people can bring questions and hear a theologically educated response, followed by open discussion. They host multidenominational community classes at the local library, high school, or community college, where immigrants or others who are new to the community can learn about Christianity. They examine the rhythms and needs of their congregants and of people in the wider community, looking for times and places where people are already gathering, where forming relationships, growth, and learning might happen. They also continually fill the gaps with short-term, long-term, and topical small-group ministries and start new classes especially designed for guests and people who are new to the faith. Churches that practice Intentional Faith Development know the secret of small groups. They build the foundations of radical hospitality and passionate worship, and from there they create multiple opportunities for intentional faith development, both inside and outside the congregation.

Learning through Experimenting

The pastor of a small, open country congregation wrestled with how best to provide opportunities for Bible study and faith formation for people who have busy family schedules and live miles from the church and from one another. Attempts to host weekday evening studies at the church brought together the same few people who always attended faithfully. The pastor supported these efforts but particularly wanted to reach some of the younger families who didn't participate as fully in such ministries. One day she shared her dilemma and desire with one of the younger families and casually asked whether the family would consider hosting an hour-and-a-half study every other week in their home if she could get a few other families to attend. The family enthusiastically agreed, and a few weeks later they had their first home Bible study on a Tuesday night in the host's living room with three other families present. The pastor led an easygoing discussion with the adults and teens about a chapter of scripture, occasionally provoking animated conversation about Jesus and his parables, and then led them in prayer together. The younger children played together in a back room. This worked so well that the pastor felt emboldened to ask another family on the other side of the county for the same favor of hosting a few others for Bible study. They graciously agreed. The pastor now leads two groups on alternate Tuesday evenings that reach about seven couples and families. Both groups then wanted to gather once every few months as a larger gathering to share dinner, Bible study, and prayers. Delight and joy energizes the conversations, and the families look forward with eagerness to their times together.

The pastor learned several lessons from her experience.

First, people desire relationships and connection and want to learn about faith, but they have trouble squeezing it into their lives. The more the church can do to accommodate and create a sense of community where people already live and work, the better.

Second, if congregations keep the end in mind (offering quality learning in community), their leaders may have to break out of usual patterns and expectations of place, frequency, and curriculum to reach people. What about the extra work of leading two studies away from the church? She answers, "What pastor wouldn't give an evening a week to teach the faith to more than 20 percent of her congregation? This is huge for us, and I only hope we can do more in the future!"

A larger church tried unsuccessfully several times to launch a young adult Sunday school class. Leaders had the tactics down right: they'd develop a list of sixty to eighty names of regular attenders, guests, and friends between the ages of nineteen and twenty-eight; they'd recruit a couple of young adults to lead and teach the class; and after much publicity, correspondence, and phone invitations, they'd host an evening dinner party before the launch of the Sunday morning class. This had worked for starting classes for other ages just fine. About twenty young adults would attend the dinner, and about fifteen would come to the first few weeks of classes, but after three months the class would inevitably dwindle to four or five people and then die out. The church repeated this pattern every twelve to eighteen months for years. They were stumped on how to get good quality teaching and fellowship going for young adults.

As they prepared for their next attempt, a married couple in their mid-fifties stepped forward to help. These "empty-nesters" had children of their own who were young adults, and they seemed unlikely candidates for teaching the class. But they were mature in their own faith, had taught classes before, and had an inviting and accepting graciousness. They felt God had nudged them toward this ministry, they genuinely loved young adults, and they promised to give the work their best time and energy. The pastor and leaders offered their blessing, and the couple set to work. They contacted young adults one by one and couple by couple to talk about their hopes for the class. They checked websites, made phone calls to other churches, and visited with other leaders of successful programs for young adults to get more ideas. They discovered that lumping college students with young couples starting families was not going to work, and they chose to focus on young couples. After weeks of personal conversations, they formed a small group to discuss plans and preferences for how to proceed. Most of the couples with young children wanted to bring their children to the opening dinner. (This pattern of preferring to include their children in as many events as possible continued for years.) The first gathering had fifty to sixty people, and the leaders described the purpose of the class, the topics they would begin with, and some of the other activities and ministries they might do together. From the beginning, the class began to demonstrate extraordinary care for one another, especially when couples gave birth or faced illness among their children. The young adults adopted an invitational stance, always searching to bring others in. Within a few months, they were looking for service projects that could use their talents and passions. The ministry launched successfully, maintained strong participation that continued to grow, developed an outward focus, and continues to serve numbers of young adults today.

Meanwhile, the church staff considered alternatives for the college-aged young adults. Early-morning Sunday school classes were not attracting the college crowd. The youth director met for lunch with several students to talk about their interests and the rhythms of college life. Late Sunday evenings, students returned to the campus area and wanted to see each other to catch up on the weekend's activities. They stayed up late anyway and were usually scrounging for something to eat. So, the youth director invited all the students to her home at nine o'clock on Sunday evening, and the students spent a couple of hours together eating, catching up, talking about questions of faith, and praying for one another. Sunday evening allowed students to reconnect after the weekend and gave them a chance to spiritually prepare for the challenges of the week to come. They decided to meet every other Sunday night at nine.

What did the pastors and staff learn through these experiences?

First, keep trying. Don't give up. Try different times, places, leaders, and formats, but keep trying.

THE MIDDLE DOORS

The pastor and staff of a mid-sized congregation noticed that while many new guests visited worship, and a good percentage of them moved toward further involvement in the ministries of the church, nevertheless worship attendance remained steady. For several years the church had seen growth in attendance, and they couldn't figure out why it was leveling off. The congregation practiced hospitality with excellence; guests and new members felt welcomed at worship. But then after a few months, guests and new members would drift away, become less consistent in attendance, and fall away altogether. To understand the situation better, the pastor visited with some members who had joined in the last several months.

He discovered that people felt welcomed and supported when they first visited and continued to feel a sense of belonging in worship. But when they tried to become part of Sunday school classes, men's organizations, choirs, and Bible studies, the groups felt cliquish and uninterested in welcoming new people. Even after months of trying, they felt at the margins in these smaller communities and ministries. One woman said, "Before I moved here, I was the kitchen chief in my previous church for years. I didn't expect to do that again here, but I hoped to join the cooking team. When I showed up to help with a dinner, they handed me napkins and told me to put them on the tables, and then I stood around by myself the rest of the evening. I felt like they didn't need me or want me."

Leaders discovered that "the front door" was working well as people felt invited and welcomed. But they were

slipping out "the back door" because they were discovering too many of the "middle doors" were shut
tight.

The staff began a series of teaching events and lessons in the adult classes, mission teams, service organizations, choirs, and Bible studies to try to move
the culture of hospitality deeper into the life of the
congregation. After some months, they noticed that
the small groups started to grow, and with them the
worship attendance began to trend up again. Most
new people will not feel like they really belong until
they find meaningful connections and relationships in
smaller groups beyond the worship experience. Are
your "middle doors" open?

Second, the secret is relationships, relationships, relationships. People
want to be treated with respect. They want to feel valued, and they hunger
for a sense of belonging. Like all adults, students want to determine their
own direction and be given responsibilities equal to their gifts.

Third, beware of lumping young adults into a single category when
there are significant differences between singles, couples, couples with
children, college students, and non-college working young adults.

Fourth, the successful leadership by the couple in their fifties helped
the staff see something they had missed before. Many young adults feel
estranged from their own parents, often because of divorce, remarriage, or
conflict while they were growing up, and yet they want to relate to people
in their parents' generation who treat them as adults and who can model a
maturing faith and the successful navigation of parenting's rough waters.
They're searching for faith mentors and models.

Finally, young adults may not have much experience in matters of
faith and may feel self-conscious about their lack of knowledge, but they
nevertheless hunger for relationship, for a deeper spiritual life, and for

opportunities to make a positive difference in the lives of others. They are suspicious of the forms of religion but are attracted by the practices of prayer, learning, and serving.

The practice of Intentional Faith Development takes a thousand forms. Some churches offer prepackaged, high-commitment learning experiences, such as Covenant or Disciple Bible Study, Alpha, or Bible Study Fellowship. Others rely on weekend retreats or one-day mini-retreats that they plan and resource themselves. Others overlay small-group work with ministry and mission and train people as congregational care ministers, pastoral care teams, visitation teams, choirs, praise bands, prayer circles, or mission and service teams. Others deepen the quality of community and learning in traditional settings such as adult Sunday school classes or women's and men's organizations. Others emphasize support groups that address critical needs such as Alcoholics Anonymous, grief support groups, parenting support groups, divorce care, elder care, or Alzheimer's family support organizations. And countless churches simply create their own setting, title, and focus, offering short-term or long-term learning academies, Lenten studies, Advent retreats, or topical studies on the Bible or on books about social or faith issues. Even small churches can offer robust ministries of learning, growing, and maturing in faith by creating new opportunities for long-term attenders and newcomers to learn in community. Churches of any size can work with other congregations or community organizations to co-host classes. They can figure out where people are already gathering, and offer short- and long-term learning opportunities there. It only takes "two or three gathered in [Jesus's] name" to experience the presence of Christ and to grow together in faith.

New Leadership

People's lives are changed through the experience of in-depth study courses and long-term Bible studies. In a church I served, after experiencing Disciple Bible Study, people began to discern their call to differing forms of leading, teaching, and serving within the church and in the larger community, and a few went on to full-time Christian service. The practice of tithing increased, worship attendance became more consistent, and people developed a deeper appreciation for the sacraments. For the next ten years, virtually all significant leadership for new children's programs, mission initiatives, faith-forming classes, worship services, and stewardship emphases came from those who had deepened their understanding of the faith through in-depth Bible study. The fundamental changes in faith and habit brought by Christ persist and become fruitful only when sustained by continual learning in community.

When everyday disciples take their own spiritual growth seriously and immerse themselves in the study of scripture, in prayer, and in fellowship, they understand the purpose of the church and the point of ministry differently. Peter Drucker has said, "The function of management in a church is to make the church more church-like, not to make it more business-like" (*Drucker and Me* by Bob Buford [Nashville: Worthy Publishing, 2014], p. 97). While leaders should apply their knowledge of business, accounting, real estate, law, and banking to enhance the church's effectiveness and accountability, they cannot lose sight of the purpose of the church, which is derived from the life, teaching, ministry, death, and resurrection of Jesus Christ. How can leaders make good faith decisions for the congregation without proper grounding in the faith? How can they operate with flexibility and creativity to share Christ with people outside the church, if they are not driven by knowledge and understanding of Christ's own other-focused life? The decision on whether or not the congregation should offer weekly worship and fellowship for recovering addicts cannot be reduced to insurance liability issues; it's a ministry decision. Whether the church should fund an overseas mission trip or launch a food truck to feed the community's homeless is a decision not reducible to a mere cost-benefit analysis. These decisions require hearts of faith that explore the will of God as well as minds that review the financial reports. Fruitful congregations are led by everyday disciples and pastors who intentionally work to grow in the grace of Jesus Christ and in the knowledge and love of God.

THE COOL CHRISTIAN DUDES

A group of men were friends and fellow disciples. They served together, enjoyed fellowship, participated in sports ministries, and even a barbecue ministry. (It is Texas, after all!) But they started feeling restless, and each sensed that he needed something more. They wanted a real connection to other men of faith, a different and deeper challenge in their spiritual life. One of the men remarked, "We want to be like a guy I work with. You just know he's a Christian by his words and deeds. He's a cool Christian dude." At about the same time, a ministry had begun at the church for young men from the community who needed a place to play basketball, blow off steam, and hang out together. The group of friends decided they needed a weekly time to study and talk about the sermon from the previous Sunday. They decided to spend time in prayer together, and to include time for sharing whatever was going on in their lives. They met once a quarter at a pizza place. Then they decided their main meeting should coincide with the Monday night basketball games so they could begin to form relationships with the younger men. The younger men could see "regular guys" taking their faith seriously, learning and growing and laughing and praying together. Their group needed a name, and they chose what they lightheartedly longed to be: The Cool Christian Dudes.

Practical Approaches

Faith communities that practice Intentional Faith Development are creative and flexible. They not only offer high-quality traditional adult classes for learning and fellowship, they also initiate and support opportunities for learning during the week and at all hours and in many places. They focus on the needs and schedules not only of the people in the congregation, but they get to know the people in neighborhoods around them and their needs and schedules, too. They innovate continually, in order to respond to people inside and outside the church. These are some ideas:

o   Offer classes on weekday evenings, before and after church services, or on weekday mornings. If your community includes people who work on shifts, offer classes timed accordingly. Throw away any notions that there is a "right time" for studying the faith.

o   Launch groups that meet in people's homes, and at cafés, in libraries, in park shelters, at yoga studios, at the community college, in a community garden.

o   Create lunchtime study opportunities at offices, plants, retail centers, or other locations where people work.

o   Ask people when and where they would like to learn and grow. Focus on the schedules and interests of the people for whom you are seeking to create opportunities, even if it doesn't fit the usual weekly church schedule or doesn't fit inside the church walls.

o   Offer study and learning groups for one-time, short-term, and long-term studies, so that people can try out a class without making a big time commitment, and so they can see what it's like.

o   Establish one night during the week as prime time for studies, and offer multiple types of classes and groups on that night. Provide a meal before classes start. It could be as simple as pizza. Or a potluck. Or participants could prepare the meal together.

o   Make sure some learning opportunities are easy-entry, with no preparation needed, and offer others that are more in-depth, requiring reading ahead of time.

o   Set a goal for how many people from the congregation will be part of some sort of study. Measure participation quarterly. Evaluate how you're doing, and look for ways to do better.

o   Continually assess the topics covered in your classes. Consider what is happening in your town, the nation, the world, and especially in the neighborhoods, schools, and workplaces surrounding your church. What are the concerns, needs, and anxieties of people there? Generate ideas for topical studies or groups focused on particular interests.

o   Advertise any opportunities for people to learn and grow. Communicate within your congregation and also reach out to people outside of the church. Use social media. Set up accounts on two or three social media outlets, and post weekly invitations and information. Always include locations and times, and your website address. Ask people in the congregation to post and share. Take photos and videos of classes having fun and sharing meals together, and post those (with permission from anyone pictured).

o   Find effective ways to connect with your congregation in order to continually remind and inform them of the ongoing and new opportunities for Intentional Faith Development. Survey the congregation to find out what methods they prefer. Set up a weekly e-mail, if congregants are receptive, and send a message preparing them for worship, sharing any news, and listing opportunities to learn, grow, or participate in the church that week.

o   Create a weekly study guide based on the sermon, with space for notes. Include scripture texts and maybe key points. Consider including a few scripture passages for further study. Include questions for reflection, and a prayer. Slip the study guide inside worship bulletins, or incorporate it into the bulletin design.

o   Make sermons available to watch online as streamed videos.

o   Make sermons available as podcasts.

o   Develop a study around bread-making, with Bible study and discussion around topics of holy communion, mealtime fellowship in scripture, or the primary symbols of the Christian faith.

o   Create a community garden, and develop classes to meet, work, and fellowship together there, including people from the surrounding neighborhood. Develop studies that focus on Jesus's agrarian parables, or plants as metaphors for spiritual growth, or the problem of sin—like weeds in our lives.

o   Run a booth at the local farmer's market, selling bread or produce from the community garden, or whatever other wares your congregation can offer. Host a conversation and meal after the market each week for anyone interested.

o   Develop the assumption in your congregation that task-oriented small groups (such as choirs, praise bands, cooking crews, and mission teams) are also about the formation of faith. Foster a culture of devotion and learning in every group and ministry team so that every gathering is laced with prayer and characterized by mutual care. Work toward the objective that every learning group includes fellowship and every gathering for fellowship includes practices that lead to faith formation.

o   Emphasize experiential learning. Create opportunities for people of all ages to learn by doing.

o   Develop a mentoring process, so that people have accountability and guidance for their spiritual growth. Invest in a system that will help you create a discipleship pathway for people.

o   Meet people where they are—physically and spiritually. Provide resources that tap into different people's interests and levels of spiritual maturity.

o   Give permission for groups to self-organize. Reduce or eliminate rules about group size, meeting schedules, and topics. Support people who wish to gather in groups of two or three, in homes or businesses or city parks or bars or anywhere. Encourage people to gather without needing to seek approval.

o   Give permission for groups to engage in experiences that may be new or unusual to others in the congregation. Support people who want to engage in prayer walking, silent retreats, yoga classes, bread-baking as a spiritual exercise, psalm-singing, praying the hours, monastic community life, and other forms of religious practice.

o   Give permission for people to gather around common interests, using those interests as an entry point for learning about the faith. Support those who want to gather around cooking, painting, dogs, basketball, dance, hip-hop, roller derby, tattoo artistry, music collections, photography, video games, movies, gardening, woodworking, junk collecting, paper-making, camping, rock-climbing, origami, vlogging and blogging, parenting, and so on. Imagine Paws for Prayer, Paws and Praise, or Pawverbs at a dog park. Have fun with names and places. Motherlode (yes, that's the name they chose for themselves!) for young mothers meeting after their children are asleep to talk about life, faith, parenting, and work or Cool Christian Dudes, for those who feel like anything but. Imagine a quilting guild that prays together, cares for one another, and makes quilts for foster care children, victims of natural disasters, or people undergoing cancer treatment. Give it a creative name, such as Peace by Piece, Piece Makers, Common Thread, or Piece Corps. How about Life Gatherings, a group of friends, family, and coworkers who work together to be more faithful followers of Christ, or a kayak or hiking or fishing affinity group who gather for work early before sunrise before encountering God's awesome creation?

o   Understand that some people may enter the life of the church through the "middle door," a small-group gathering focused on Intentional Faith Development. For some, worship on Sunday morning can be intimidating or off-putting. A one-on-one or small group conversation is the safest and most accessible entry point to exploring faith. Support those who are part of your community who have the compassion to engage with others in this way. Release the need to control their experience or to push them along toward greater involvement. Be OK with the reality that each person's faith develops differently. Create and protect the space and time for that to happen, inside and outside of your congregation.

Growing in Grace

Pastors and staff members of churches that value Intentional Faith Development not only publicly support and help lead Bible studies and classes, they also highlight the importance of continuing faith development in sermons, lessons, and online articles. They express as much concern for people growing in the fullness of faith as in crossing the threshold at the beginnings of faith. Even when the language of sanctification is not explicitly used, themes of maturing in faith recur in the core values of the congregation. The notion of growing in grace becomes widely known, highly valued, and broadly practiced.

Congregations that practice Intentional Faith Development are not afraid of failure and willingly initiate ministries of learning in community, knowing that some will take root and last for a generation and others will continue only a few months and then fade away. They don't allow those who have no interest in the topic, time, or setting to veto those who are interested and willing, and so they're not afraid to start groups with low numbers, trusting that God will make use of the time to help those who participate.

Congregations that excel at Intentional Faith Development rely not only on their pastors to lead teaching and formation ministries, but they especially invite, support, and prepare non-clergy leaders to teach Bible studies, form communities, and coordinate support groups. They charge people with the task of getting to know their neighbors, other families at school, coworkers, and people they encounter outside of the church. Mission-minded disciples pay attention and discern the needs and questions of their neighbors, and they look for opportunities to form authentic relationships.

These congregations take seriously the care and nurture of teachers, volunteers, and other servers, supporting them with appreciation, resources, and training. They lift leaders in prayer, recognize them in worship through consecration or appreciation services, and send personal notes of encouragement. They develop systems to see no one feels alone, unequipped, or unappreciated. They develop searchable curriculum lists, to make it easy for leaders to find resources. Congregational leaders readily support formal training by paying costs for required workshops and seminars.

Churches shaped by Intentional Faith Development know the value of taking people away from their daily lives for one- to three-day retreats to focus on the spiritual life. They develop overnight retreats for women, men, couples, youth, and families, for people who are part of the congregation and those who are not. Purposes range widely, from Advent and Lenten retreats to topical events with guest speakers. They use books and special resources and include times of learning, reflection, fellowship, sharing, worship, and quiet.

The pastor and staff also practice learning in community. They attend to their own faith. Pastors study Scripture not only to prepare sermons but also to deepen their relationship with God. They participate in forms of community with other pastors or everyday disciples through lectionary studies, covenant groups, or learning networks. People sense that their pastor is growing, learning, and deepening in faith.

Churches that practice Intentional Faith Development know that maturation in Christ is always about content and relationship. Ideas change people, and people change people; and God uses both together to work on our behalf and to shape our lives in the image of Christ. Transformation comes through learning in community.

Congregational leaders that practice Intentional Faith Development carefully consider the full life cycle and look for ways to form faith at every stage. They look for gaps and opportunities and unmet needs both inside and outside their congregations. They inventory their complete annual program of ministry for elementary-age children: Sunday school, children's choir, mid-week programs, summertime activities, Christmas programs, children's church, children's mission project, and all other ways they touch the lives of children during the year. They ask themselves if their ministry is sufficient, full, helpful, and effective. They ask how they can do better. In similar fashion, they consider preschool children, youth, college students, young adults, singles, couples, middle-aged adults, and seniors. They look outside at the neighborhoods and communities around them. They talk with school administrators, civic leaders, nonprofit agency staff, business leaders, health care providers and others who are involved in the community to find out what would be helpful and engaging for people who are interested in learning more about Christianity. They honestly assess how they are doing in providing opportunities to form small learning communities to sustain growth in the faith at every stage of life. Rather than providing haphazard, hit-and-miss, eclectic formation ministries, they seek to cultivate growth in faith in more intentional ways that address unmet needs and invite more and more people into formative relationships.

The Work of the Holy Spirit

The embrace of Christ deepens our sense of belonging through the practice of Radical Hospitality. God turns our hearts and minds toward Christ through Passionate Worship, gracing us with the desire to follow Christ more nearly. The practice of Intentional Faith Development matures our understanding and experience of Christ. The transformation of human hearts and minds is God's work through the Holy Spirit. Intentionally learning in community is our way of placing ourselves in the hands of God so that God can sculpt our souls and re-create us in the image of Christ. Doing so alongside people who are new to us, who are not part of our inner circle of friends, or in places that are outside the four walls of our church—perhaps even in places where we're uncomfortable—requires great intention, but results in unimaginable growth of faith and a flourishing of the fruit of the Spirit. The refreshing intimacy and companionship of Christians learning together engrafts us onto the body of Christ and becomes a means of grace by which God awakens a heightened desire to love our neighbors. Interior spiritual renewal and growth changes outward behaviors as following Christ becomes a way of life. The growing desire to serve Christ by loving our neighbor creates an eagerness to respond to the call of God to works of mercy, compassion, and justice. This leads us to the next practice of fruitful congregations, the practice of Risk-Taking Mission and Service.

CONVERSATION QUESTIONS

List small-group ministries that help people to form relationships as they study, learn, experience, and practice the faith. How is faith nurtured for children? Teenagers? Young adults? People who are new to faith?

How does your congregation encourage non-clergy everyday disciples to form small communities in places away from the church to give people opportunity to form relationships and explore faith?

GROUP ACTIVITY

In groups of two or three, share what you most want to learn about the faith. Who are mentors you'd like to learn with to experience learning through serving, and what are the settings that are most favorable to you for learning?

Consider the people in your own neighborhood—their lives, backgrounds, and schedules. What might they want to know or learn about, related to the spiritual life? And what would you like to know or learn about other people's spiritual journeys? What are convenient times and neutral spaces where you could gather? Who might you connect with to start a conversation about this possibility?

Chapter Five

The Practice of Risk-Taking Mission and Service

"Truly I tell you, just as you did it to one of the least of these who are members of my family, you did it to me." (Matthew 25:40)

Two people, a married couple, actively belonged to a faith community in New Braunfels, Texas. They experienced the typical ups and downs of life, and found their faith tried and tested, like most of us. Through the years they listened, paid attention to the whisper of God, the stirrings of the Holy Spirit nudging them along the path of discipleship. They learned to be open-hearted toward other people, curious and respectful, and had become more and more comfortable engaging with people from various backgrounds. They studied and formed relationships with others in the congregation, actively pursuing a deeper spiritual life. And they loved to worship God. Worship grounded, rooted, challenged, and nourished them.

This couple began to experience a particularly strong nudging, both of them around the same time. It was a question, nagging and persistent: Where do the homeless people in our community go each day? Who are they? How do they live, and where do they find shelter? They had seen people who had no homes, but when they asked around they were told "there are no homeless in New Braunfels." The couple kept asking questions and eventually learned why, technically, that was true. Most of the homeless were routinely picked up and taken outside the city limits and left there.

The couple persisted, still asking those questions. How do they live? Where do they go? Eventually they found small camps located near the interstate, under the bridge of the Guadalupe River, and behind abandoned buildings. Emboldened by their faith and their spirit of openness, they drove up to the camps, got out of their cars, and gently approached the men and women. In each of those first encounters, the couple asked simply, "What do you need?"

Socks. Underwear. Food. Batteries. The couple brought those items to the camps and stayed to visit. They listened and shared stories. There were awkward moments and beautiful ones, and laughter. They began to form relationships. Every Saturday they went in search of people their community did not want to see.

They began to wonder if they might help in other ways, too. Specifically, they wondered if their friends without homes would like to participate in prayer or worship or even Holy Communion. This idea was welcomed. So, they asked their pastor to come. She did. They worshipped and prayed and shared in the sacrament. They gathered again and again. The people in the camps, the couple, the pastor, and a few other everyday disciples from Gruene United Methodist Church decided to make worship under the bridge a regular monthly event. Someone made a promotional flyer, printed copies, and handed them out at the camps and around town.

At 8:45 on Saturday morning, a small team of people from the congregation met at the church to load the trucks with tables and chairs, breakfast and coffee, a generator and music equipment. They carried boxes of clothing, collected earlier in the week as an offering for their homeless neighbors. Folks had also gathered that week to assemble bags of food, enough to last a person for a few days. Those bags were loaded up, too. Someone from the music team created song sheets, and made copies so that anyone who wanted to could participate. Musicians showed up with their instruments. A person from the congregation had prepared a brief message, and arrived, notes in hand. The elements for Holy Communion were carefully packed and loaded in the back of a car. These folks who attended the church, others from the community, and people without homes from the various camps all made their way to the designated location, beneath the interstate, along the river's edge. There they had church. There they *were* the church.

A LITTLE EFFORT BY MANY

At one congregation, people take their vow of service seriously. Folks are asked to devote one hour per week to serving in the community. That amounts to nearly six hundred hours of Christians offering help and hope for their neighbors. A little effort from many people has a huge impact.

Imagine how awkward those first moments together must have been for everyone. What would you say and what would you do if you found yourself in a similar situation?

The next month, on the appointed Saturday, something unexpected happened. The trucks were loaded, song sheets copied, message written, food bags and communion elements all prepared. The people from outside the homeless community arrived and were met by a welcoming party made up of their homeless friends. They had left their homeless camps early that morning and gathered at the worship site. They swept the dirt to remove all the cigarette butts, emptied the trash, and made their space ready. They worked elbow-to-elbow with people from the church to unload the trucks. They set up tables and chairs. It took off from there. The people who lived in the homeless camps took on the task of welcoming people before worship; they became the greeters. They distributed the flyers, inviting people to their church by the river. They enlarged the circle of worshippers, inviting people who slept in their cars, and the working poor

OPEN THE EYES OF OUR HEARTS, LORD

Bee Creek United Methodist Church is situated in an affluent area outside of Austin, Texas. They have a heart for outreach. They send teams to areas hit by disasters, to the inner city to repair homes, and to Guatemala to serve an orphanage. Nevertheless, they had no idea the depth of need a few miles from their front door.

A nurse in the congregation checked out an elementary school in another district, across the river. What she learned was hard to believe. Just twelve miles from the church, children lived in homes without enough food, reliable electricity, or even running water.

When she shared this news with leaders, everyone sat in stunned silence. How could this be? They'd heard of "pockets of poverty," but never really connected it to real people who were their neighbors.

In worship and leadership meetings, they began to talk about the school, the students, and their needs. The congregation wanted to help.

First, they prepared and distributed hygiene packs, hosted a health fair, and provided school supplies and shoe vouchers. Then they built a community garden behind the library to augment the canned and frozen food available at the local crisis ministry. A civil engineer and a retired computer programmer offered to work on the problem of how to bring running water to these homes. The congregation is not finished, but their eyes are now open to their neighbors.

who simply couldn't make ends meet. Many weeks earlier, that couple from the church just *knew* there were people living without homes in their town, and they decided to serve God by helping them. Those very people were now welcoming *them*, singing songs of praise, praying, and receiving Christ with *them*, serving God by helping others as brothers and sisters with *them*.

The relationships grew over time, centered in the monthly Saturday morning worship experience. The communities of people attending mingled and overlapped. People who attended the church started to recognize two very important unmet needs in the communities of people without homes: showers and laundry. Showers were available at a truck stop, but cost fifteen dollars per person for one shower. And everyone needed a place to wash clothes. Many people had jobs but no homes, and usually slept in their cars; those folks certainly needed a way to clean their clothes. The church was in the process of building a new space for their expanding food and clothing ministries. The pastor and leaders decided to add two family restrooms equipped with showers, and to make them fully accessible, so that adults with disabilities or mobility issues could use them. They also added two washer and dryer sets to their building plans. The ministry is open four days a week, and is staffed completely by volunteers, providing food, clothing, laundry, and showers. And people gather for Church by the River Saturday mornings once a month, brothers and sisters serving God and each other in moments that are still sometimes awkward. And very often beautiful.

The story of worship under the bridge illustrates an important aspect of the Five Practices. They are, now more than ever, intertwined and integrated fully into the life of congregations. This is perhaps most strikingly true in the case of Risk-Taking Mission and Service. Missions and outreach ministries were, for a long time, viewed as separate programs, largely disconnected from the lifeblood of the church. These ministries were self-contained offshoots, events one could sign up for like you might sign up for a shore excursion as part of a cruise. An excursion, not the main journey. For any congregation seeking to be fruitful, those days are over. Radical Hospitality, Passionate Worship, and Intentional Faith

Development all lead to and are fueled by Risk-Taking Mission and Service. Each Practice shapes and builds on the others. We see that in the example above, where two people embody the Practice of Radical Hospitality, are inspired through Passionate Worship, and nurtured by Intentional Faith Development until they are moved by the Holy Spirit to pursue a Risk-Taking act of Mission and Service.

The Changed Life

It is risky to bring together people from different parts of the world, different walks of life, and even different neighborhoods of a city with the attendant inequities of wealth and power and so many other differences. Paternalistic and patronizing attitudes can spoil good intentioned efforts; assumptions of cultural supremacy poison honest learning; ignorant and insensitive words, dominating personalities, and self-righteous attitudes create chasms between people, making matters worse.

On the other hand, such projects done well and with the proper spirit absolutely change lives. Teams of volunteers build homes, construct churches, repair parsonages, erect wheelchair ramps, establish clinics, provide medical care, paint schools, dig wells, widen roads, and teach children. They focus on the relationships and people, rather than on materials and buildings, and achieve a level of genuine engagement, of mutual listening and learning. This sort of Risk Taking Mission and Service requires an openness and vulnerability, which feels risky for just about anyone. To stretch ourselves requires the risk of discomfort.

Mission initiatives change the lives of those who receive the help. One woman who lost nearly every earthly possession in a flood said, "I didn't cry when the water destroyed my home. But when I saw people traveling from so far away to help me clean up and rebuild, I couldn't stop crying." Nothing is as hard as a lonely struggle, and discovering that others care enough to help, to give their time, to work hard, to sacrifice on another's behalf is a touch of grace. This work changes lives. A cinderblock house with a concrete floor replaces houses of patchwork boards with no floor at all, vaccinations and antibiotics prevent suffering, newly dug wells save people from miles of hard daily walking, ramps and wheelchairs make a way for people to participate in their communities, releasing them from the imprisonment of a homebound life. Never underestimate the transforming power of small actions. God uses caring and effective people in every circumstance to improve other people's lives in a multitude of ways. We are each made to serve the other.

Hands-on mission and service changes the lives of those on the receiving end, and those on the serving end. Nobody walks away after serving others and looks at his or her own life in the same way. When we are part of these encounters—when we listen and learn about the people we are serving, when we are open to new experiences and new ideas—we find a light shining back on our own lives. We see our own habits and values in new ways. Our misguided or ignorant assumptions are illuminated. We recognize our own extravagance, consumerism, materialism, and wastefulness. Perhaps we see the ways we participate, knowingly or by default, in institutionalized injustice and in systems that perpetuate inequity. Countless pastors have discerned their call to ministry through active engagement with people on service projects. Retired people have rededicated their lives to a new purpose after experiences serving others, and college students have changed career paths because of the impact of face-to-face, hand-in-hand mission work.

Mission initiatives change churches. Even when a small percentage of the membership immerse themselves in significant mission and service, the texture of church life changes, and the language of service and outreach begins to form conversations and priorities. Ministries of mercy and justice take root. Tolerance increases; youth activities evolve beyond parties, movies, games, beach trips, and amusement parks; and these ministries become focused on changing lives and making a difference for the purposes of Christ. The interweaving of lives across culture, class, color, and age boundaries genuinely enriches the congregation and makes Scripture stories come alive in real experience. God strengthens the body of Christ through mission and service, and God empowers the body of Christ through witness.

IT'S ABOUT MORE THAN ROOFS AND FLOORS

A predominantly Anglo congregation held an annual home repair and construction project in poorer neighborhoods to build wheelchair ramps, replace roofs, and redo plumbing and flooring for people who did not have the resources for such things. The work focused on a predominantly Hispanic neighborhood, and for three days the targeted homes turned into work sites with dozens of volunteers arriving in SUVs, holding their Starbucks cups, unloading high-cost tools, taking cell phone photos, and playing music while they worked. Team members noticed that the family they were serving retreated more from the site and the workers each day. They became concerned about how the people who lived in the homes felt about this experience.

This motivated the planners to solicit Hispanic sociology students from a nearby university and contract with them to do a follow-up visit to each of the families they had worked with over the previous several years. The students compiled an assessment tool to evaluate what the experience had been like for the families to receive work teams. They conducted their surveys in Spanish without church people present. Families reported feeling a loss of control about their homes, self-consciousness and embarrassment with their neighbors about receiving help, rejection at their efforts to assist in the repairs, and awkwardness about language limitations. They appreciated the work completed on their homes, but during the experience, they felt in visible as people talked about them in their presence. Based on these responses, leaders radically revamped the ministry with far greater sensitivity and respect for the families they serve, more intentional personal engagement, and mutual conversation in the residents' native language throughout the project. Even the best-intentioned projects can benefit from the analysis, "How do we build goodwill and positive relationships as well as buildings?"

Fundamental to the Mission of Christ

Risk-Taking Mission and Service includes the projects, the efforts, and work people do to make a positive difference in the lives of others for the purposes of Christ, whether or not they will ever be part of the community of faith. Congregations increasingly focus their efforts locally, zeroing in on the points of need in their own communities, in the neighborhoods surrounding their church or in the area where they gather. Many congregations also practice Risk-Taking Mission and Service by sending work teams to locations outside their own region, to other states or overseas. Many develop teams of people who are equipped and trained to respond and rebuild after natural disasters and other catastrophic events. Others get involved with senior adults in retirement centers or assisted living facilities, or with people who are incarcerated or recently released from prison, or with women who have been victimized by human trafficking, or with people who are recovering addicts who live together in accountability communities, or with people of all ages with differing mental and physical abilities. In many instances, these groups of people are included in the regular rhythms and habits of the church, and participate fully as members of Christ's community. No congregation can do *all* of these types of ministry without spreading itself too thin. Fruitful congregations increasingly focus their energy and resources on what is truly in front of them—the deepest needs of local people.

Risk-Taking Mission and Service is so fundamental to church life that failure to practice it in some form results in a deterioration of the church's vitality and ability to form disciples of Jesus Christ. When congregations turn inward, using all resources for their own survival and caring only for their own people, then spiritual vitality wanes and the mission of Christ suffers.

The Calling to Serve

Ordinary Christian service takes many forms. Keeping the church alive and fulfilling its purpose requires the active and regular service of everyday disciples. The impulse to serve, animated by the spirit of God in Christ, causes people to give time generously to help with ushering or parking, assist in the kitchen, sing in the choir, serve on planning teams, visit homebound or hospitalized people, teach a class, help with children's ministry, transport youth, take gifts to first-time visitors, help with cleanup around the church. Such basic and ordinary service is the lifeblood of the body of Christ. The phrase "to equip the saints for the work of ministry" (Ephesians 4:12) means that faith communities encourage, prepare, and cultivate such ordinary service so the ministry of Christ thrives. The operations and ministry of a congregation require the cooperative and helpful spirit of everyday leaders who love the church and want to see it run smoothly and effectively to fulfill its mission, and the fruit of their service includes community formation, connection to one another, and changed lives for those within and beyond the congregation. Fruitfulness is also evidenced by tasks that are done well, by people working together effectively. A church whose people do not offer generous and willing service will never practice Radical Hospitality, Passionate Worship, Intentional Faith Development, or Extravagant Generosity since these depend upon the leadership, time, effort, prayers, sweat, and tears of faithfully committed people. The responsibility falls to all who love the church to use their talents and energy. Making ourselves useful for the purpose of building the body of Christ imbues our lives with purpose and connects us to others. Genuine and generous service makes a difference.

The word *mission* turns our serving outward. Mission reminds us that Christ's compassion, grace, mercy, and love extend to the entire world, and these fruits are cultivated not only within the walls of the church or among the people of the body of Christ who are regularly seen and already known. Mission refers to the positive difference made in the lives of people beyond the inner circle of the church. Mission bears witness to our faith by exemplifying the compassion, mercy, and justice of Christ in the world.

Rooted and Grounded in Scripture

Offering oneself in deliberate service to improve the conditions of others is rooted in more than three thousand years of faith tradition. Nothing is more central to faith identity and to the church's mission than transforming the lives and conditions of people by offering oneself in God's name. Nearly every page of scripture shows people serving God by serving others.

The earliest scriptures record a consistent emphasis upon justice, compassion, respect, and love for the neighbor. The books of law not only restrain violence, fraud, theft, and harm but call us to "love [our] neighbor as [ourself]" (Leviticus 19:18). Scripture inextricably links love of God to love of neighbor and calls people to charity, justice, and mercy. The Psalms reveal the nature and intent of God in passages replete with reminders that God is the "lover of justice" (Psalm 99:4); that God "loves righteousness and justice" (Psalm 33:5); that the people of God are "to do justice for the orphan and the oppressed" (Psalm 10:18); and the people are to "give justice to the weak and the orphan" (Psalm 82:3). The theme continues in the writings of the prophets, "He has told you, O mortal, what is good; and what does the LORD require of you but to do justice, and to love kindness, and to walk humbly with your God?" (Micah 6:8).

Jesus echoes the words of the prophets to describe his purpose: "The Spirit of the Lord is upon me, because he has anointed me to bring good news to the poor. He has sent me to proclaim release to the captives and recovery of sight to the blind, to let the oppressed go free, to proclaim the year of the Lord's favor" (Luke 4:18-19). The stories of Jesus consistently point toward God's love for the poor, the sick, the outcast, and those most vulnerable to the oppressions of society. Against the resistance of the religious elite and contrary to the advice of his disciples, Jesus lifts up the bent-over woman on the Sabbath, touches the unclean with healing power, releases the paralyzed from his bed, eats with tax collectors in their homes, and risks the violence of the mob to intervene for the woman accused of adultery. In teaching and action, he reveals that God's way includes costly demonstrations of unexpected love for the least likely. The stories of the good Samaritan, the father risking humiliation to welcome back his prodigal son, and the rich person neglecting Lazarus at his own doorstep all consistently show who Jesus is; and through Jesus, we see what God intends for us.

When have you witnessed someone offering a costly demonstration of unexpected love? How was God at work in what happened?

Jesus tells us that in every act of compassion, people touch Christ. "I was hungry, and you gave me food, I was thirsty and you gave me something to drink, I was a stranger and you welcomed me, I was naked and you gave me clothing, I was sick and you took care of me, I was in prison and you visited me" (Matthew 25:35-37). The disciples can't imagine what he is talking about, until Jesus says, "Truly I tell you, just as you did it to one of the least of these who are members of my family, you did it to me" (Matthew 25:40). And Jesus demonstrated the posture he asks of his followers by washing his disciples' feet, taking the form of a servant. Directly addressing servanthood, Jesus says, "Whoever wishes to be great among you must be your servant . . . the Son of Man came not to be served but to serve" (Matthew 20:26-28).

The life of service flows naturally and inescapably from the teachings of Jesus Christ, and no congregation or disciple can avoid the direct gift and demand of God's call to love and serve others. A faith community without service dies like a tree with neither roots nor fruit, without nourishment or purpose.

Compassionate service marked the early church as disciples were admonished to "be doers of the word, and not merely hearers" (James 1:22).

They prayed for the sick, visited the imprisoned, and marshaled their resources to provide for the needs of the poor. Paul recognized how the core practice of love defined the Christian life, "If I speak in the tongues of mortals and of angels, but do not have love, I am a noisy gong or a clanging cymbal. And if I have prophetic powers, and understand all mysteries and all knowledge, and if I have all faith, so as to remove mountains, but do not have love, I am nothing" (1 Corinthians 13:1-2). Love, incarnate in ministries of compassion, mercy, and justice, bears witness to the living Christ.

The Stretch of Christian Discipleship

So, if mission and service appropriately describe the volunteer impulses and outward reach that characterize so many of our congregations, why qualify them with the adjective *risk-taking?* Fruitful, growing congregations push beyond ordinary service and everyday missions to offer extraordinary opportunities for life-changing engagement with people. This characteristic of Mission and Service is more important than ever.

Risk-Taking steps into greater uncertainty, a higher possibility of discomfort, resistance, or sacrifice. Risk-Taking Mission and Service takes people into ministries that push them out of their comfort zone, stretching them beyond the circle of relationships and practices that routinely define their faith commitments. God uses such ministries to bring people together, causing people to experience situations, needs, and especially relationships that they would never ordinarily have and that reveal to them spiritual qualities and practical talents that, apart from their deliberate intention of serving Christ, they would never discover.

Jesus says, "If you love those who love you, what credit is that to you? For even sinners love those who love them. If you do good to those who do good to you, what credit is that to you? For even sinners do the same" (Luke 6:32-33). People naturally love those who love them. Anyone with the good taste and good sense to treat me well is the kind of person I find it easy to treat well in return! People instinctively love their families and friends, those who think and live like they do, those with whom they naturally intermingle and congregate. Even unbelievers and those who never seek Christ do the same. The social cohesion of countless good political associations, civic clubs, professional organizations, neighborhood cliques, trade unions, and country clubs prove the point.

The stretch of Christian discipleship is to love those for whom it is not automatic, easy, common, or accepted. To love those who do not think like us or live like us, and to express respect, compassion, and mercy to those we do not know and who may never be able to repay us—this is the love Christ draws out of us. Jesus stepped across oppressive social boundaries, intermingled with those who suffered crippling infirmities and social stigma, and offered hope to those at their point of gravest despair. He loved the least lovable and the most vulnerable, and he offered the same unmerited grace to the greatest sinner as to the finest saint. The down-and-out see in Christ as much love for them as the up-and-coming. And Christ invites his disciples to follow him into this kind of love.

"But love your enemies, do good, and lend, expecting nothing in return. Your reward will be great, and you will be children of the Most High; for he is kind to the ungrateful and the wicked. Be merciful, just as your Father is merciful" (Luke 6:35-36). "Do to others as you would have them do to you" (Luke 6:31).

RABBITS FOR WIDOWS

Children from one congregation partnered with an agency to send Angora rabbits to widows in Rwanda. The kids raised money and (along with other churches) helped purchase rabbits and supplies and get them sent overseas. The rabbits' wool can be made into yarn and sold or into items that are sold to provide a small income for the widows. The ministry sends pictures, snippets of rabbit wool, and a video of an ultrasound of the bunnies when they start to breed. The ministry forms wonderful relationships that stretch across the globe.

Risk-Taking Mission and Service involves work that stretches people, causing them to do something for the good of others that they would never have considered doing if it were not for their relationship with Christ and their desire to serve him.

Ask, "What have I done in the last six months to make a positive difference in the lives of others that I would not have done if it were not for my relationship with Christ?" Reflecting on this question takes us to another level in our understanding of Christian discipleship, and points us toward real Risk-Taking Mission and Service.

Risk-taking also draws our attention to the truth that many of our most urgent ministries have an uncertain, unpredictable quality. We cannot know whether or not our efforts will make the difference we hope. Much of our hardest work may have little visible impact or may seem to end in utter failure. Sometimes alcoholics we help through rehab return to addictions, children we remove from violent homes run away anyway, homes we build are destroyed by the next flood, disadvantaged youth we support with scholarships drop out after two years, and ex-cons we take a chance on end up back in prison. Like the seeds scattered by Jesus's sower that land on rocky ground, get choked by weeds, or gobbled by birds, many of our finest efforts come to no visible good. But like Jesus's parable promises, as we remain faithful to the task, a harvest comes forth in miraculous ways. Christ's ministry requires our willingness to risk failure.

The Risk with Following Christ

Risk-Taking now becomes more than merely an adjective intensifying what we mean by Mission and Service. Risk is an integral part of following Christ. The world is changing. We encounter new people, in new circumstances, on a regular basis. Fifty, twenty, or even fifteen years ago, much of a congregation's Mission and Service was done in places and with people who were at least somewhat familiar and perhaps similar to the members of the congregation. The typical exception was an overseas mission project. Generally, we were serving people who spoke the same language, with whom we had common life experiences. Now, because of the widening gulf of inequity among Americans, people living in the same city have dramatically different living conditions, education, health care, access to technology, access to transportation, and access to nutritious food. Elements one person might consider basic essentials for life may be unimaginable for a person who lives one zip code away.

Add to this the ever-diversifying, richly varied demographic pool, with people of many different ethnic origins, nationalities, and religious traditions all living, working, and attending schools together. In the not-too-distant past, we could generally assume that anyone we encountered in the US had at least a baseline knowledge of the Christian faith, plus baseball, apple pie, and the American Way! That baseline American experience provided a risk-mitigating safety net of sorts. We are aware of it now because it has mostly disappeared. Many of us experience a sharper sense of "risky" now.

There is less certainty about the world and how to serve in it. We are less sure of the rules, and we often don't understand the language. Or the food. Or the clothing, family customs, or religious traditions. And so, with such wildly disparate life experiences, risk is now inherently and more dramatically part of Mission and Service. Is it possible that others perceive our feelings of caution or uncertainty or even fear? And if they do, does that recognition shape their notions about us, and about Christ?

Risk-Taking Mission and Service requires time. It is less project-oriented and more long-term, developing naturally, sometimes beginning with no particular end or objective in sight other than to build relationships. It requires conviction. Family and friends may not understand or support the work, and may resent the time it takes. Risk-Taking Mission and Service requires vulnerability. We must be open to *receiving* help, sometimes from those we are aiming to serve. We open ourselves to learning, to seeing God in new ways through another person. We drop our assumptions and remake our responses. We turn our suspicion into curiosity, our hesitation into hopefulness, our self-protection into self-disclosure. Grace becomes our driving instinct.

Risk-Taking Mission and Service requires us to release the need for control. When a congregation "owns" a project, start to finish, it is easier and more cost-effective. We adhere to a budget and run on a schedule. We can do service projects with precision, if that's our aim, modeling our missions after TV home makeover shows with massive teams rolling in with trucks full of tools and supplies, timetables and megaphones in hand, overrunning the worksite with speed and efficiency, while the homeowners (or people "being served") are politely removed to a safe distance. This is not what "Go and Do" means.

"Go and Do" means listening, learning, forming relationships long-term. It means doing mission *with* and *alongside* rather than *for* or *to* others.

Attentiveness to People Around Us

David, a pastor serving in various ministries for years, after conscientious prayer and study, concluded that capital punishment runs contrary to the teachings of Christ. He also realized how controversial and unpopular this perspective was in his own community. Protesting publicly and signing petitions did not fit his style. Instead of trying to win consensus in his church about capital punishment (although he unapologetically teaches what he believes) and feeling frustrated by the intransigence of the criminal justice system and legislature to change, he decided to make his own personal commitment. By patiently working through the resistance of the bureaucracy of a prison near his home, he received permission to make biweekly pastoral visits to one of the prison's death-row inmates. Every other week, he submits to the searches, completes the forms, and signs the waivers so that he can spend an hour in conversation, reading, Bible study, and prayer with a man convicted of murder who has no appeals, no options, and no hope as the world understands it. He does this consistently and without publicity or need for recognition. He holds no naïve hope of conversions or reprieve. He simply and graciously steps into the world of another person radically different from his own to offer the ministry of Christ. It's a world he would never know and never consider entering if it were not for his relationship to Christ.

After their children went off to college, four women from a suburban congregation decided to move beyond their comfort zone with their serving spirit. They took a one-day training for literacy tutors, contacted the pastor of a church in an area with low-income housing and a high drop-out rate, and were introduced to several children and their mothers seeking basic literacy and English-language classes. Each Friday, the four spent two hours teaching, listening, laughing, crying, and otherwise interweaving their lives with people they would otherwise never have come to know. They supported one another, worked as a team, made contacts that drew their own congregation into greater engagement with the church, and felt God's Spirit reshaping their perceptions about poverty, race, and language. It was a world they would never have considered entering if it were not for their relationship with Christ. Later one of the women said, "I didn't want to do it, but God pushed me through the door. I receive more than I give. Now I wouldn't trade my time with these young people for anything."

The history of mission and service consists of successive excursions from the same starting point and along a similar trajectory: listening, observing, attentiveness to the people and situations around us. A growing and intentional awareness of human need. Perceiving God's call to do something. Feelings of unworthiness and inadequacy. More listening and observing, now *with* the people we serve. Asking questions, participating in their own assessment of the need, learning what they would like to see happen. Taking time, nurturing relationships, earning the right to serve, earning trust. Employing spiritual gifts and material resources. Overcoming resistance. Opening ourselves to suffering. Partnering with others to make a difference. Recognizing our *own* need. Allowing others, even those whom we serve, to serve us, to alleviate our need. Discovering meaning and purpose in a life with Christ. Inviting others.

Many Ways to Serve

In the body of Christ are many members, and "not all the members have the same function" (Romans 12:4). Those who courageously and faithfully take on bold or audacious ministries for the sake of Christ require much support and encouragement. People who are not able to manage great risk can serve in other ways, by providing financial resources and management, cooking, serving meals, doing graphic design and printing, offering media creation, setting up and cleaning up for events, marketing through social media and communication of all types, praying, planning events, assembling supplies, providing musical leadership and worship design, offering transportation, training others, writing notes of encouragement, and so on.

The sharp edge of new and bold ministry often begins with the leadership of a few people, brings others into supportive roles, and then engages the whole congregation. Fruitful congregations encourage, support, and embolden those who are imaginative and adventurous in their engagement with the sufferings of the world, and then cultivate systems that help many more people use their talents and resources to make a difference. Such congregations invite, involve, and shape the altruistic, self-giving stirrings and callings of everyday disciples.

Never underestimate the enormous impact a congregation can have, even if only a small percentage of people offer themselves for front-line, risk-taking service. Even major projects begin by God calling only one or two people to do something bold.

Bold ministries of Risk-Taking Mission and Service find their beginnings not just in individuals but in Bible studies, planning teams, youth ministries, or women's or men's organizations. An amazing number of long-established community-wide women's shelters, literacy centers, ESL programs, family clinics, immigrant legal services, crisis centers, schools, children's homes, and hospitals began because a group of people encountered a situation or heard a speaker or read an article or watched a video about suffering or injustice, and the people collectively decided to do something about it. They felt the call of God and poured themselves into the task, invited others to join and support, collaborated with other churches and community leaders, and formed a ministry to make a difference in the lives of thousands. Even the most audacious and robust community ministries began small, with a group of committed believers as common as the ones you worship and study with weekly.

Christ brings people out of themselves and into the lives of others where they would never have gone on their own. One congregation sent one or two teams each year to clean up churches and homes after tornadoes and hurricanes. As the teams grew more confident, developed more skill, attended more training, and cultivated greater leadership, one of the teams applied and was approved as a first responder. Now, they are not only prepared to help with clean-up during the weeks after a disaster, they are prepared to arrive first, providing immediate essentials of food, water, housing, and emotional support. Their work has blessed countless families. During each mission, the congregation surrounds them in prayer and sustains them with financial support for the equipment, travel, and expenses of this extensive ministry. The trained volunteers are not EMS technicians or firefighters but ordinary teachers, office workers, cashiers, truck drivers, lawyers, and retired folk who have let Christ push them out of their comfort zone and put them face-to-face with human suffering and need.

Go and Do

Faith communities that practice Risk-Taking Mission and Service raise money to support overseas, international, and community work, absolutely. But they pour the greatest energy into developing relationships with people and organizations in their local area. They ask what is needed, and they listen. They discern how to collaborate and participate in service work that is already happening, and how to serve with other people. They create opportunities in places all over the community, where people can plug into the action of serving their neighbors. They organize teams, train volunteers, and send people to work directly in hands-on, face-to-face ministry. They spend time in reflection periodically, to process all that is happening and to find ways to improve. They understand that failure will be part of the experience. They focus on learning, especially learning from people whom they serve. They open themselves to being served. They value long-term relationships, and they measure the impact of their work in lives changed rather than in money sent or buildings constructed. They don't stop at reading about the global church; they globalize their own ministry by forming partnerships with sister churches, supporting student exchanges, and sharing common prayers. Faith communities that practice Risk-Taking Mission and Service give people multiple opportunities to serve, to belong to a community that matters, and to change lives. They go, and do!

Such congregations put forth the effort to see that the people they serve feel respected, confirmed, confident, and blessed, not dependent or helpless or indebted. They do *mission with* people of other cultures and not *ministry to* them; they don't view service as a one-way street, as if they hold all the answers and have all the resources and are helping people who have nothing. They sharpen their sensitivity to the inequalities of power and wealth, and work toward partnerships and mutual ministry in which they learn as much as they teach, receive as much as they offer, and grow in Christ through their sharing of Christ's compassion. They practice humility and cultivate the fruit of the spirit in their work together with those they serve. They expect nothing in return and do not hunger for public approbation or measure their impact by the gratitude expressed by those they help. People come first.

Congregations shaped by Risk-Taking Mission and Service not only solicit and encourage ordinary service to support the work of the congregation—inviting, equipping, organizing, encouraging—but they also consciously motivate people to more extraordinary service. They lift examples in preaching and teaching, and they support those on the cutting edge of service with prayer, funding, and appreciation. They don't let the fear of controversy or resistance override their support for ministries of compassion by members called to such work. They do not self-righteously criticize or belittle those who cannot or will not work on the front lines beyond the comfort zone, but rather they develop ways in which everyone can play a supportive role. The spirit of mission unites them rather than divides them. They don't try to make everyone fit the same mold, and they offer mission and service opportunities with gradations of involvement and differing levels of complexity appropriate to the talents, skills, and interests of a variety of people. They don't just promote the highly visible, time-intensive special projects but also provide ways for those who can give a few hours a week to serve. They value the person standing atop the roof on the work-site as highly as the person writing letters to the legislature at home, realizing that each is serving in his or her own way. For the person who steps forward wanting to serve, there is always a place.

Such congregations not only support volunteers who serve on church-sponsored projects but also encourage service with community agencies, civic organizations, hospitals, clinics, schools, rehab centers, and prisons.

Helping people in Christ's name is not merely the prerogative of adults but is a regular part of the formation of children and youth. All youth and children's ministries—weekend, weekday, and summer activities, and retreats and camps—include teaching and experiential components that stretch compassion outward beyond the walls of the church. Youth ministries practice age-appropriate, hands-on, in-person service. They invite medical workers, teachers, and project team members who have returned from international work to present programs for young people to enliven interest in the global family. They pay a stipend for college students to intern during the summer to work on mission projects. Faith mapped in childhood provides pathways that shape lifelong commitments. Churches with too few students of their own collaborate with other congregations to offer cross-cultural, hands-on service opportunities that help people, reshape attitudes, and form memories.

Churches that practice Risk-Taking Mission collaborate with other denominations, civic organizations, social agencies, and nonprofit groups. They form alliances and cooperate to provide a wider array of services. They partner with businesses to bring the greatest possible resources to bear to address particular human needs. They share responsibility and credit as long as quality, integrity, and effectiveness are preserved.

Such congregations make space for people who do not attend church to make a difference in the lives of others. Serving experiences become an entry point into the church and into life in Christ. People with no religious affiliation yearn to improve the conditions of other people by relieving suffering, reducing poverty, or struggling against injustice, but they often hold an image of churches as self-serving and self-absorbed, or as hypocritical. Service isn't just for insiders and long-time members; it's a means God uses to shape faith and bind people into the body of Christ.

Missional congregations streamline the process by which ministries are approved, supported, and completed. They replace lengthy and rigid organizational protocols that strangle passion with a more permission-giving environment that is agile, quick to recruit and respond, and empowering of those who passionately want to serve. They use technology to facilitate service. They knock down the obstacle of distance by using video conferencing for meetings; they develop relationships with people across the globe, who become partners and collaborators. They shoot videos and photos to share on social media, at worship, and at other gatherings. They utilize digital platforms for project management and training. They learn new languages, practicing daily with language apps. They continue annual and ongoing projects that truly make a difference, and they work to create additional channels of service so that the church's ministry remains fresh, new, and relevant to the changing needs of the community and world.

Congregations that practice Risk-Taking Mission and Service realize that while feeding one person at a time, building one house at a time, and counseling one prisoner at a time are vitally important, churches also have a responsibility to bear witness to wider social change. They tend to legislative policies, changes in public funding, legal proposals, and business practices with an eye for protecting the most vulnerable. Remembering Jesus's particular compassion for the poor and powerless, they advocate for policies that improve the lives and conditions of those who struggle at the margins of society. They mobilize against racism, injustice, and abuse, and they work and pray for peace. They stay informed about issues that affect people and encourage civic and political participation. Risk-taking witness is a tool God uses to change lives, communities, and nations.

Seedlings for Consideration

o   Study a language that will help you engage with people in your area. Perhaps do this with others from the faith community. Consider offering ESL classes or reciprocal language learning (where English-speakers teach English and Spanish-speakers [for instance] teach Spanish).

o Offer classes to help people earn their GED at the church, library, or community center.

o Learn about asset-based community development, and use this concept to shape Risk-Taking Mission and Service. Ask people in a community, "What is great about this neighborhood? What is great about the people here?" Start with the resources, skills, and positive attributes of the community itself, and build from there.

o Spend time just being with people in the community. Allow relationships to develop naturally:

  – Make and share meals together.

  – Do Bible study or explore other topics together.

  – Work in a community garden together, and share the flowers and produce.

  – Trade lessons—teach each other how to cook or sew or make something that's special in your culture or family.

  – Watch sporting events, like the Superbowl, World Series, or World Cup together on TV.

  – Work on cars or bikes together, sharing tools and skills.

o Set aside feelings of blame or guilt. Perhaps you did not create the problem, but you can decide to take responsibility for helping to solve it. Use resources like books, videos, and speakers to facilitate healthy, respectful conversations. Open pathways for communication. Find ways to ease tension, to lift the weightiness of differences in language, perspective, and life experience.

o Be OK with awkwardness.

o Support foster children and foster families. Ask agencies what children and families need. Offer events where people can learn more about fostering. Host parties for foster kids. Support foster families with meals, supplies, and other needs.

o Launch a bookmobile to serve children in your area. Run it with volunteers. Stock it with donated books. Establish a regular schedule of stops, so that kids and schools can count on new books each month.

o Start a food truck ministry to serve hungry people in your community, especially those who cannot or will not go to shelters for meals.

o Offer a mobile health clinic in a truck or a pop-up health clinic, setting up in spaces throughout the community where people are in need.

o Install showers in your facility for people who have no homes. Install washing machines and dryers for people who have no access to laundry facilities.

o Train people to serve as care ministers. Give them theological, psychological, and safety training to prepare them for service in prisons, assisted-living centers, women's shelters, refugee detention centers, rehab facilities, schools, and elsewhere.

o Establish partnerships with a school. Work with the parents, teachers, and administrators to find out what they need and how best to provide it. Paint school rooms. Build a playground. Invite people to serve as tutors, readers, and mentors. Load backpacks with healthy food for children to take home for the weekend. Provide school supplies. Host room parties. Surprise teachers with gifts. Host a health fair for schoolchildren and their families, with free screenings. Distribute hygiene kits for kids and parents.

o Spread peanut butter and jelly throughout your town! Launch a peanut butter and jelly ministry in offices, shops, and other businesses where people pack lunches for the homeless during their lunch hours once each week.

The Distinct Call of God

What's the opposite of risk-taking? Safe. Predictable. Comfortable. Certain. Convenient. Fearful. These words do not describe the ministry of Jesus Christ who said, "For those who want to save their life will lose it, and those who lose their life for my sake will save it" (Luke 9:24). Congregations are not ends in themselves; they are resources God uses to change lives and transform the world.

God places congregations in a world troubled by many challenges. Schools struggle to provide basic education, and many children fall through the cracks. Criminal justice systems are overcrowded and do little to restore people to functional, positive participation in society. Medical services are overburdened and unprepared to serve unmet needs, especially of the poor, the uninsured, and the unemployed. Immigration policies and environmental threats intensify fears. Drugs, alcohol abuse, gambling addictions, family violence, and unmitigated poverty rob people of hope. A majority of the people with whom we share the world live with incredible uncertainty because of poverty, hunger, illness, or war.

As followers of Christ, we cannot live as if these things have nothing to do with us. Christ moves us closer to suffering, not farther away. We cannot walk around obvious suffering, ignoring it and denying it like those who preceded the Samaritan down the road to Jericho. We can't moan about how somebody ought to do something. We cannot merely lift those who suffer in prayer, asking God to do for us what God created us to do for God.

Faith communities that practice Risk-Taking Mission and Service are dissatisfied and offended (for Christ's sake!) by the abuse of children, the suffering of innocents, the oppression of the poor, the mistreatment of immigrants, racism and hate speech, and the recurring cycles of addiction, violence, and injustice around them. They hear in the human need of their neighbors the distinct call of God. Against all odds, they figure out a response and offer themselves faithfully and genuinely, even at some cost to themselves. They ask questions, listen, collaborate, and learn. God uses them to transform the world.

Congregations form disciples by graciously offering the Radical Hospitality of Christ so God can reshape lives through Passionate Worship and deepen faith through Intentional Faith Development. In such congregations, people discover the call of God to make a difference in the lives of others through Risk-Taking Mission and Service. To sustain these practices so that the body of Christ thrives requires the Extravagant Generosity of Jesus's disciples, and it is to that practice that we now turn.

CONVERSATION QUESTIONS

What is the most unexpected place to which your faith in Christ has taken you in order to make a difference in someone's life?

How do you suppose your congregation is perceived by those in the community who have the least power—the poor, the unemployed, the stranger, the hungry, the homeless, the abused, the addicted, the immigrant, the victim of violence?

How are relationships formed between those who belong to the faith community and those the community seeks to serve? Where do you see collaboration and partnership about preferred outcomes?

GROUP ACTIVITY: WALKING THE NEIGHBORHOOD

Select a geographic area in your town, one where a small group of people can safely walk, covering most of the area on foot. In groups of three or four, walk the area. Record your observations and sensations in writing on paper or on your phone.

As you walk, Listen, Look, and Smell.

What do you see? What do you not see?

Who do you see? Who do you not see?

What else do you observe? Use your senses.

What questions or wonderings arise from this experience?

Follow the questions that arise. Pray about them. Do the questions lead you to a point of pain or injustice? To a point of hope and possibility?

What can you do to learn more?

Chapter Six

The Practice of Extravagant Generosity

"You will be enriched in every way for your great generosity."
(2 Corinthians 9:11)

I'd feel better if we could go over it one more time," Matt told his wife, Keri, as they worked together preparing their talk for the next day's Generosity in Giving service. Before they practiced their presentation again, they found themselves reminiscing about the last several years and the incredible faith journey that had brought them to this point. The next morning they would share their story about their step-by-step movement toward tithing. Just a few years ago they couldn't have imagined doing something like this.

Matt and Keri grew up in families that attended church. Though they attended youth ministries, they were less active during college. After meeting each other, getting married, and settling into the community, they became involved with a congregation once again. Now they're in their mid-thirties with two young children. They're both professionals with moderately high incomes, even though Keri works part-time while the children are young.

Matt and Keri had attended Bible study together. The experience deepened their desire to learn more about the faith and to offer more of themselves in service. They helped begin a class for people their own age, providing much of the initial hospitality. They have also helped with children's ministries, mission projects, and countless fellowship events. They love their church. Most of their closest friendships have developed through belonging to a community of faith.

Five years earlier, the pastor invited Matt and Keri to write a short devotional about giving. Generosity in Giving Sunday is the culmination of the church's financial campaign each fall. Pledges made during that season are collected on Generosity in Giving Sunday, and will support the following year's ministries. The invitation caused them to think about their giving. They felt good about the amount of their annual gifts and believed that they were giving generously, more than most couples their age. The Generosity in Giving campaign emphasized proportional giving with the goal of tithing. When they did the math, they realized that they were giving less than 2 percent of their annual income to God's purposes through the church. They began to explore the practice of the tithe with greater interest.

Even though they prayerfully studied the biblical roots and practices that supported the tithe, giving 10 percent simply seemed too much to expect. They had a mortgage, car payments, college savings, and retirement plans to think about. They never had money left over at the end of the month. How could they possibly tithe?

Matt and Keri prepared the devotional that year based on their reflections about Jesus's story of the widow who put two coins in the treasury, giving more than all the others because she gave out of her poverty. They wrote about how they and their fellow churchgoers give out of abundance rather than poverty, and they challenged others to grow in giving. They also decided to increase their giving by half that year, pushing them toward 3 percent of their income.

The next year, Matt and Keri were asked to give announcements in church about Generosity in Giving, talking about how giving shapes their faith. That was the year they accepted the challenge of growing toward the tithe. They increased their giving by another 1 percent and decided to do that each year for several years until they tithed. Giving 4 percent involved rethinking personal habits. They looked at some of their spending patterns, such as how frequently they bought fast food rather than eating together at home, the number of years they drove cars before replacing them, and the kinds of entertainment they did together as a family. This level of giving caused them to look at other financial matters, including their saving and investing. They made subtle, positive changes in their lifestyle. One day it occurred to Matt that their salaries usually increased by about 4 percent per year. If they saved and spent half that increase each year and used the other half to increase their giving, they could reach the tithe in three more years. That's what they did, even though they faced one year when their income slipped lower. They kept growing in their giving as a proportion of income.

Matt and Keri reached the full practice of tithing. As much as they had prayed, talked, read, and committed themselves to the tithe, nothing prepared them for the first time they actually wrote a check for 10 percent of their income and gave it to the church at the beginning of the month. Keri remembers it as a "gut check moment" in their faith journey. It seemed crazy and extravagant. They also enjoyed an incredible sense of gratitude toward God.

Five years after that first devotional in the church newsletter, Matt and Keri were asked to share about their journey of faith and their growth in the grace of giving. They felt privileged and humbled to share but didn't want to boast or appear self-righteous. While the journey toward tithing had been satisfying personally and spiritually satisfying, it had not been easy.

In planning their presentation, they decided that Matt would tell about how the tithe had deepened their practice of faith. People talk about putting God first and having God at the center of their lives, but in actual practice most of a person's major decisions are made without reference to God's will or priorities. God is really peripheral instead of central. Instead of giving God the leftovers at the end of the month, tithing is a spiritual discipline that puts God first. It's a practical way of saying, "God really is Lord of our lives." Tithing takes enormous trust in God. Tithing strengthens faith.

Next, Keri would describe how tithing forced them to think about the use of money and how all they receive has been entrusted to them by God.

Tithing made them spend money more wisely, with less waste and fewer superfluous purchases. Practicing the tithe caused them to save more diligently and to consider the impact their investments have on society. They looked at their money as if each dollar had a mission. As stewards, their job was to see that the money fulfilled purposes consistent with their being followers of Christ. How they spent, how they saved, and how they gave reflected this sense of mission. Tithing made them rethink their borrowing and debt. Lowering credit card and auto debts freed substantial amounts for saving and giving.

For Keri and Matt, tithing had broken the sense of panic, worry, desperation, and fear that had driven many of their financial decisions in the past. The knowledge that they could willingly give away 10 percent of their income relieved their feeling trapped, paralyzed, or hopeless about their financial situation. They worried less.

The journey had enriched their relationship immeasurably. Giving generously forced significant discussions about their goals and values as a family that they would never have had otherwise.

Finally, they would close their witness by describing how tithing intensified their engagement with the mission of the church. They became more keenly involved and interested in the well-being and fruitfulness of the faith community than they ever had before. They delighted in the fruitfulness of its ministries. They made the church's mission part of their own and prayed for the people, the ministries, and the outreach of the church with renewed passion.

Matt and Keri reviewed their talk one more time, overwhelmed by the awesome sense of change that had come over them during the last several years. They offered thanks to God as they looked forward to sharing their story in order to encourage others to grow in the grace of giving.

Generosity Enlarges the Soul

With minor variations, Keri and Matt's story has been repeated in the lives of countless followers of Christ. First-century Christian communities, the Methodists and other Protestants of the 1700s, faith mentors, and models of Christian living today—all have discovered a truth as sure as gravity, that generosity enlarges the soul, realigns priorities, connects people to the body of Christ, and strengthens congregations to fulfill Christ's ministries. Giving reflects the nature of God. Growing in the grace of giving is part of the Christian journey of faith, a response Christian disciples offer to God's call to make a difference in the world.

Keri and Matt's steps toward tithing are similar to my own, and their journey resonates with the stories of innumerable Christians of all walks of life—janitors and teachers, factory workers and small business owners, maids and executives, lawyers and farmers, wage earners and retired folks, doctors and work-at-home moms—some with incomes so small that it's difficult to imagine how they manage to give anything at all, and others with resources so large that their faith community can't absorb their generosity, causing them to direct their charitable impulses toward clinics, colleges, new church starts, and social service agencies.

People who give generously do so because they genuinely desire to make a positive difference for the purposes of Christ and because they want to align their lives with higher purposes. They give in response to the Spirit's urging and feel a soul-sustaining satisfaction in the sense of meaning and connection that comes with generosity. They give because they love God, love the church, and desire to grow in love of neighbor.

Fruitful congregations practice Extravagant Generosity. They teach, preach, and practice proportional giving with a goal toward tithing. They encourage people to grow in giving as an essential practice of Christian discipleship, and as a faith community they practice generosity by their extraordinary support for missions, outreach ministries, and organizations that change people's lives. They thrive with the joy of abundance rather than starve with a fear of scarcity. They give joyously, generously, and consistently in ways that enrich people's souls and multiply the ministry impact of the church.

As people grow in relationship to Christ, they grow also in the practice of Extravagant Generosity, offering more of themselves for the purposes of Christ and providing the resources that strengthen ministry and that help the church touch the lives of more and more people in the same way their own lives have been transformed by God.

Scriptural Roots

Scripture is replete with examples and teachings that focus on possessions, wealth, giving, gifts, generosity, offerings, charity, sacrifice, and sharing with those in need. Giving is central to Jewish and Christian practice because people perceive God as extravagantly generous, the giver of every good gift, the source of life and love. People give because they serve a giving God.

In the Old Testament, numerous passages underscore the significance of tithing (giving a tenth) and of first fruits (offering the first and best of the harvest, livestock, and income to the purposes of God). In Genesis 14:20, Abram gave a tenth of everything to God, and throughout Leviticus and Deuteronomy, the practice of tithing and first fruits is evident. The book of Exodus says, "Take from among you an offering to the LORD; let whoever is of a generous heart bring the Lord's offering" (Exodus 35:5). Offering money and other possessions to God results from generosity of heart rather than from mere duty and obligation.

In Proverbs, people are reminded to "Honor the Lord with your substance and with the first fruits of all your produce" (Proverbs 3:9). How people use their material resources either honors or dishonors their relationship to God. Generosity aligns one's life with God's purposes.

The prophet Malachi calls upon people to rely genuinely upon God by offering the tithe, implying that when people test God's faithfulness, they find God's presence and promises trustworthy (Malachi 3:8-10). The voices of the prophets ring the warning that people cannot expect material sacrifices alone to please God but that God's reign requires justice, righteousness, and faithfulness (Amos 5:21-24; Micah 6:8).

Jesus's teachings abound with tales of rich and poor, generous and shrewd, givers and takers, charitable and selfish, faithful and fearful. He commends the poor widow putting her two coins in the treasury; giving out of her poverty, she "put in all she had to live on" (Luke 21:4). The story upsets expectations by pointing to proportion rather than amount as the measure of extravagance.

In the story of the farmer who built bigger barns, placing his trust too much in earthly possessions, Jesus asks the spiritually probing question, "And the things you have prepared, whose will they be?" He warns, "Take care! Be on your guard against all kinds of greed; for one's life does not consist in the abundance of possessions" (Luke 12:20, 15). Acquisitiveness does not foster life rich in God.

And Jesus recounts the parable of the three servants entrusted with varying talents to illustrate God's desire for the faithful to use what has been given to them responsibly and productively. The steward who fearfully hoards and buries his talent for safe-keeping is rebuked (Matthew 25:14-30). How people use what they have matters to God.

Jesus chastises the scribes and Pharisees for hypocrisy because they tithed while neglecting justice, mercy, and faithfulness. People of God are to practice justice and compassion without neglecting the tithe (Matthew 23:23). The tithe does not meet in full measure what the gift and demand of God's grace requires of Jesus's followers.

Jesus's unexpected love for Zacchaeus so radically changes the tax collector that he gives his wealth to the poor and to those whom he has wronged. Giving serves justice and is a fruit of Christ's transforming grace (Luke 19:1-10).

Even the story of the good Samaritan highlights extraordinary generosity. The Samaritan not only binds up the wounds of the stranger left to die in the road, but he takes the stranger to an inn, pays for the stranger's care with his own money, and commits himself to provide for the long-term well-being of the stranger by telling the innkeeper, "When I come back, I will repay you whatever more you spend" (Luke 10:35). The Samaritan's generosity, like Christ's compassion, knows no bounds.

Beyond all the teachings, parables, and stories, the followers of Jesus see in the gracious and costly gift of his sacrifice and death the ultimate self-revelation of God. The most memorized Scripture of the New Testament expresses the infinite nature of God's gracious love revealed in the gift we have received in Christ. "For God so loved the world that he gave his only Son" (John 3:16).

In the early church, the followers of Jesus "would sell their possessions and goods and distribute the proceeds to all, as any had need" (Acts 2:45). Generosity was a mark of the Spirit's power to change lives and practices.

Paul describes generosity as one of the fruits of the spirit, alongside "love, joy, peace, patience, kindness . . . faithfulness, gentleness, and self-control" (Galatians 5:22-23). He describes how "we have gifts that differ according to the grace given us," including "the giver, in generosity" (Romans 12:6, 8). All Christians practice generosity while some are particularly gifted by the Spirit to give in extraordinary measures.

Paul commends the generosity of communities of faith, especially those who remain surprisingly extravagant in their giving during difficult travails. Writing of the churches of Macedonia, he says "for during a severe ordeal of affliction, their abundant joy and their extreme poverty have overflowed in a wealth of generosity on their part." They "gave according to their means, and even beyond their means, begging us earnestly for the privilege of sharing in this ministry to the saints" (2 Corinthians 8:2-4).

Paul warns those with material means not to set their hopes on the uncertainty of riches but rather on God, who richly provides everything. "They are to do good, to be rich in good works, generous, and ready to share, thus storing up for themselves the treasure of a good foundation for the future, so that they may take hold of the life that really is life" (1 Timothy 6:18-19).

In every Scripture above—Abram with his tithe, the widow giving all she had, Zacchaeus in his transformation, the Samaritan with his compassion, the Macedonian church during its travails, and God's self-giving in Christ's death and resurrection—giving is always extravagant, life changing, and joyous.

John Wesley and the early Methodists practiced generosity as an indispensable aspect of discipleship, essential for the maturing of the soul and for the work of the church. Wesley taught Methodists to "gain all you can, save all you can, and give all you can" ("The Use of Money," 1744). He feared that the frugality of early Methodists would lead to levels of wealth that would distract them from their growth in faithful living. Wesley warned against earning money in destructive ways, by means that corrupted the soul or contributed to injustice. He encouraged people to live simply, without opulence, avoiding the waste of money on things unnecessary. Early Methodists were invited to practice self-control, self-restraint, and self-denial. Such practices deepened faith, avoided pride and vanity, and resulted in a greater capacity to help others. Generosity, according to Wesley, was rooted in grace, an emptying of oneself for others, an expression of love of God and neighbor.

Exceeding Expectations

The practice of generosity describes the Christian's unselfish willingness to give in order to make a positive difference for the purposes of Christ.

Extravagant Generosity describes practices of sharing and giving that exceed all expectations and extend to unexpected measures. It describes lavish sharing, sacrifice, and giving in service to God and neighbor.

Fruitful, growing congregations thrive because of the extraordinary sharing, willing sacrifice, and joyous giving of their members out of love for God and neighbor. Such churches teach and practice giving that focuses on the abundance of God's grace and that emphasizes the Christian's need to give rather than on the church's need for money. In the spirit and manner of Christ, congregations that practice Extravagant Generosity explicitly talk about the place of money in the Christian's walk of faith. They view giving as a gift from God and are driven to be generous by a high sense of mission and a keen desire to please God by making a positive difference in the world.

The notion that stewardship rightly focuses on the Christian's need to give rather than the church's need to receive is not simply a money-raising strategy but a spiritually powerful truth. The practice of tithing blesses and benefits the giver as much as it strengthens mission and ministry.

Americans live in an extraordinarily materialist and consumerist society. We are immersed in a culture that feeds acquisitiveness, the appetite for more and bigger, and that fosters the myth that self-worth is found in material wealth and that happiness is found in possessing. Thirty-year-olds feel like failures because they don't already have the kind of house and car that their parents own, and forty-year-olds feel unsuccessful because they're not millionaires. Millions of couples struggle under oppressive levels of debt that strain marriages, destroy happiness, and intensify conflict and anxiety. As one radio show host says, "We buy things we don't even need with money we don't even have to impress people we don't even know" (*The Dave Ramsey Show*).

Many Americans spend more than they earn each year. The Great Recession (2007–2012) may have slowed that trend, and other destructive financial habits, for a time. But old patterns return over time, and lessons are forgotten. Many people sustain their outbalanced lifestyles through ever-increasing auto loans, credit card debt, and mortgages.

When people with different incomes are asked, "How much more income would it take for you to be happy?" they answer in surprisingly consistent ways, saying that 20 percent more income would ease their burdens, help them buy all they needed, and bring security. People earning $10,000 think an income of $12,000 will finally bring happiness, and those earning $50,000 think that with $60,000 they can finally get on top of things, and those earning $500,000 feel that with only $100,000 more income, they will finally have it made! In other words, people who earn 20 percent less than we do think they will be happy if they can earn what we earn. So why do we feel discontent with what we have? Happiness based on possession causes people to pursue a receding goal, leaving them dissatisfied, wanting more, and never able to satiate their desires.

At root, these are spiritual problems, not merely financial planning issues. They reveal value systems that are spiritually corrosive and that lead to continuing discontent, discouragement, and unhappiness. We can never earn enough to be happy when we believe that satisfaction, self-definition, and meaning derive principally from possessions, and we can never trust our sense of self-worth when it rests on treasures that are material and temporal. A philosophy based principally upon materialism, acquisition, and possessions is not sufficient to live by, or to die by. At some point, followers of Jesus must decide whether they will listen to the wisdom of the world or to the wisdom of God.

As in Keri and Matt's experience, proportional giving and tithing force people to look at their earning, saving, and spending through God's eyes. It reminds them that their ultimate worth is derived from the assurance that they are children of God, created by God, and infinitely loved by God. God's eternal love revealed in Christ is the source of self-worth; true happiness and meaning are found in growing in grace and in the knowledge and love of God. Giving generously reprioritizes lives and helps people distinguish what is lasting, eternal, and of infinite value from what is temporary, illusory, and untrustworthy. The discipline of generous giving places people on the balcony, helping them look out at the consumerist society with new perspective, better able to see its traps, deceptions, and myths. The practice of generosity is a means by which God builds people up, strengthens their spirits, and equips them to serve God's purposes.

Tithing helps the followers of Jesus understand that all things belong to God and that, during their days on earth, followers are entrusted as stewards to use all they have and all they are in ways that glorify God. What Christians earn belongs to God, and they should earn it honestly and in ways that serve purposes consistent with being followers of Christ. What Christians spend belongs to God, and they should use it wisely, not foolishly, on things that enhance life and do not diminish it. What they save belongs to God, and they should invest in ways that strengthen society. What Christians give belongs to God, and they need to give generously, extravagantly, and conscientiously in ways that help others and that strengthen the body of Christ.

One hundred fifty years ago, if your great-grandparents were active in the faith, they tithed. Why were they able to tithe 150 years ago, but we have trouble doing it today? Because they were so much wealthier than we are? The truth is precisely the opposite. We struggle with tithing because our hearts and minds are more powerfully shaped by our affluence. We find it harder to give extravagantly because our society's values shape our perceptions more than our faith's values do.

ONE OF MY OWN

A long-time member and proud grandfather stood at the baptismal font with his family for the baptism of his baby granddaughter. Another infant from another family that was new to the congregation was baptized at the same service. Following the service, the two families intermingled at the front of the sanctuary as they took turns having their pictures taken. At one point, the mother from the new family needed to get some things out of her bag, and the grandfather from the other family offered to hold her baby. Other people were mixing and greeting, and several commented on the grandfather with the baby, and he found himself saying several times, "Oh, this one isn't mine; I'm just holding him for a minute."

Monday morning the grandfather called the pastor and said he wanted to see him right away. The pastor assumed the worst, thinking somehow the grandfather was upset about something from the day before. When he arrived at the church office, he told the pastor, "I want to change my will to include the church, and I want to talk to you about how to do that." The pastor was stunned and couldn't help asking about what brought him to this decision. The older man's eyes grew moist as he said, "Yesterday I realized something while I was holding that other baby, the one from the family that just joined the church. I kept telling people that wasn't my child, but then it dawned on me that the baby was part of my family, part of my church family, and that I have a responsibility for that little boy just like I have for my own granddaughter. I've been a member of this church for more than forty years, and in God's eyes I'm a grandfather to more than just my own. I've taken care of my own children with my will, but I realized I also need to provide for the children of the church. So, I want to divide my estate to leave a part to the church as if the church were one of my children." Those who practice Extravagant Generosity have a God-given vision and faith to plant seeds for trees whose shade they will never see.

Those who are new to the journey of faith may find the practice of tithing extremely challenging. They should take it one step at a time and grow into it over a few years. If they are so overwhelmed by debt that they struggle under an oppressive anxiety, they should first make the changes in spending and lifestyle that grant them freedom from excessive debt. (See *Money Matters: Financial Freedom for All God's Children,* by Michael Slaughter [Abingdon Press, 2006].) When they breathe more freely, they can begin to give proportionally, and grow in the grace of giving toward the tithe.

On the other hand, those who have been active in the church for twenty, thirty, or forty years and have attended worship faithfully and studied Scripture in classes and felt sustained by the relationships formed through belonging to a faith community and offered themselves in countless ways to serving, but who do not tithe . . . I would simply challenge them to think seriously and prayerfully about why this is. Why are the other practices of the faith relevant and helpful to them, but the discipline of tithing is not? Is the avoidance of tithing a fruit of faithfulness, or the result of submission to the values of a consumerist culture?

Practice the tithe. Teach children to spend wisely, to save consistently, and to give generously. Let them learn it from their parents and grandparents so that they will be generous and not greedy, giving and not self-indulgent, charitable and not self-absorbed. Extravagant Generosity changes the life and spirit of the giver.

The practice of Extravagant Generosity also changes faith communities. Churches that nurture proportional giving and tithing thrive. They accomplish great things for Christ, offer robust and confident ministry, and have the resources to carry out ever new and helpful missions. They escape the debilitating effects of conflict and anxiety that are the fruit of a scarcity mentality. They prosper for the purposes of Christ and make a difference in the lives of people.

Every sanctuary and chapel in which we have worshipped, every musical instrument that has given voice to the deepest longings of our hearts, every pew and chair where we have sat in worship, every prayer garden or labyrinth where we have walked, every communion cup from which we have partaken, every space where we have gathered to study scripture with friends, every ounce of flour and yeast that formed communion bread to feed us, every song that has lifted our hearts, every window framing a view of our world and mission field, every floorboard or tile or blade of grass where we have knelt to pray as people gathered by God—all are the fruit of someone's Extravagant Generosity. We have been the recipients of grace upon grace. We are the heirs, the beneficiaries of those who came before us who were touched by the generosity of Christ enough to give graciously so that we could experience the truth of Christ for ourselves. We owe the same to generations to come. We have worshipped in sanctuaries that we did not build, and drunk from wells we did not dig (Deuteronomy 6:11). And so to us falls the privilege of creating sacred spaces for others where we shall never worship.

Generosity is a fruit of the spirit, a worthy spiritual aspiration. Generosity is the opposite of selfishness, self-centeredness, and self-absorption. To practice Extravagant Generosity requires self-control, patience, kindness, faith, and love of God and neighbor. These build us up, equip us for life and for ministry, and foster perspectives and attitudes that are sustaining, enriching, and meaningful. Giving changes both the giver and the church.

A Different Approach

One congregation's giving remained level for years even though the church had enjoyed moderate growth in participation and attendance.

Since the congregation continually initiated new ministries, the budget came under increased pressure, and leaders grew more anxious. They decided to reevaluate their stewardship practices. For years, the congregation had held an October emphasis on financial commitments, highlighting the pledge to support the church with "prayers, presence, gifts, service, and witness." Each week the pastor preached on one of these pledges. At the end of the series, people completed cards pledging their time, talent, and service to various ministries. They also completed an "estimate of giving" card, specifying the amount they intended to give to support ministries for the following year.

With consensus that old ways were not working well, the pastor and the finance committee began to look at new models to develop a culture of generosity. They read books on giving, and they reviewed stewardship plans, packages, and kits. After much discussion, they agreed to common values. First, they would not use guilt, fear, scarcity, or shame to coerce people to give. They wanted people to feel good about giving and about growing in generosity. They wanted to unite and energize people and make them feel engaged with the ministries of the church. Second, they would shift more responsibility for discussing giving from the pastor to non-clergy disciples and would invite people who practice proportional giving and the tithe to give witness to growing in their faith and in their relationship to God. Third, while they would be forthright and transparent about the church's budget and financial needs, they would emphasize the Christian's need to give rather than the church's need to receive. Fourth, they would teach the scriptural practice of tithing and proportional giving, giving according to one's means.

Leaders encountered resistance from a few members who believed the church shouldn't talk about money. One person feared that emphasizing the tithe would scare people away. Nevertheless, the finance committee supported the recommendations.

The new approach involved preparing several letters inviting people to attend during October and especially on the last weekend for the celebration of Generosity in Giving Sunday. Everyday disciples were recruited to plan events and to get word out to classes and groups through social media and word of mouth. Rather than just giving information and inviting people, leaders shared about the place of giving in their own faith journeys. The plan also called for the pastor to preach on giving, generosity, and tithing during October, emphasizing the Christian's need to give as well as clearly connecting giving to the mission of the church and to the lives changed by its ministries. At a leadership dinner, people were asked to invite friends, family, and coworkers to participate in the Generosity in Giving focus and to join in a celebration lunch. At one service, someone presented a chart to show the patterns of giving for the congregation and encouraged people to take one step up toward tithing. Throughout the weeks of preparation, people shared in classes, fellowship groups, and ministry teams about why they give, how they have grown in giving, and how this has affected their relationship to God. Some people wrote brief blog posts, which were shared online and through other media. On Generosity in Giving Sunday, a non-clergy leader preached at both services about the significance of giving in the Christian life and about the mission of Christ. People completed pledge cards during the service, dedicating them to God's service with prayer. Afterward, everyone attended a barbecue lunch together. There were activities for youth and children so that they, too, could be engaged with the practice of giving.

The congregation discovered that designating one Sunday for gathering and consecrating gifts united and strengthened the church. People felt affirmed and positive about their growth in generosity, and more people than ever before increased their giving as they stepped closer to the practice of the tithe. Pledges increased by more than 30 percent from the previous year's giving. The more significant benefits were the renewed fellowship, faith, and purpose that Generosity in Giving inspired.

No congregation of any size can justify the failure to offer a high-quality, positive, spiritually sound, annual emphasis to stimulate growth in giving and provide the discipline of pledging for people to support the mission of the church. No church can allow one or two negative voices on a finance committee to dampen giving by 30–40 percent by vetoing plans for a thorough campaign. Annual pledge drives, done well and with a solid spiritual basis, benefit the givers as well as the church's ministry.

Annual plans for large churches may include high-quality printed material; videos that connect giving to mission; memorable themes, signs, and logos; and planning committees to prepare worship, music, dinners, communications, and work with children and youth. Small churches work on a different scale, requiring much person-to-person and group-by-group contact and conversation. The keys to effective and spiritually strengthening campaigns are the same in all churches, large and small: an unapologetic but gracious emphasis on proportional giving and tithing, an emphasis on giving in the giver's walk of faith, a focus on the connection of money to a compelling and clear sense of mission, widespread participation in planning and leading, and a heavy reliance not just on the pastor but on leadership from among the congregation's everyday disciples.

A Better Approach

Churches that practice Extravagant Generosity don't talk in general terms about stewardship; they speak confidently and faithfully about money, giving, generosity, and the difference giving makes for the purposes of Christ and in the life of the giver. They use God's name accurately by appealing to the highest of life-giving purposes for giving rather than employing fear, guilt, pressure, and shame as motivation. They speak of joy, devotion, honoring God, and the steady growth of spirit that leads to greater generosity. They don't apologize, whine, groan, act embarrassed, or feel awkward as they encourage people to offer their best to God. People delight in giving. Pledge campaigns are not about money, dollars, and budgets but about mission, spiritual growth, and relationship to God. Stewardship efforts deepen prayer life, build community, unite people with purpose, and clarify mission. People feel strengthened and grateful to serve God through giving.

Extravagantly generous congregations emphasize mission, purpose, and life-changing results rather than shortages, budgets, and institutional loyalty. They provide a compelling vision that invites people to give joyously, thereby finding purpose, meaning, and satisfaction in changing lives. They know that God moves people to give in order to find purpose and to accomplish things for Christ. They connect money with mission.

Ideas for Deepening Generosity

o Create high-quality annual pledge opportunities, setting the expectation for wide participation, excellent preparation, and numerous opportunities for involvement and leadership.

- Pastors lead through preaching, teaching, and personal example.

- Extravagantly generous leaders are prominent participants throughout the campaign, sharing testimonies in worship, leadership talks in classes and other gatherings, writing brief devotionals for the newsletter or website, and even delivering sermons.

- People tapped for leadership speak with integrity because of their own personal growth in the practice of giving.

- Leaders include people of diverse ages, incomes, and backgrounds.

o Focus on giving during the season of annual pledging, but also emphasize generosity throughout the year in preaching, Bible studies, classes, and other gatherings, wherever they take place.

o Regularly express appreciation to people who give. Thank givers collectively and personally, and give God thanks for increases in giving. The pastor sends personal notes of appreciation for special gifts and for unexpected increases in giving or pledging.

o Teach, model, and cultivate generosity among children and young people. Sunday school classes, after-school children's ministries, summer activities, and youth gatherings all offer opportunities to give individually and to work together in groups to achieve a ministry goal that is significant, tangible, and compelling.

o Connect the action of giving to the work of God. Encourage conversation and reflection about responsible earning, spending, saving, and giving. Use hands-on experiences whenever possible, to make the lessons tangible and memorable.

o Provide parents with practical ideas, guidance, and simple tools to foster generosity for children and youth of all ages.

o Invite young adults into leadership and enlist them in planning. Consider the patterns of earning, spending, and giving between the generations.

o Experiment with new methods for receiving gifts and pledges based on the habits of people in your community, and especially based on the habits of younger people in your community.

o Invest in high-quality technology that will allow the congregation to receive funds via text message, online banking, digital wallets, and whatever other platforms are widely used in your area. How do you receive offerings in a time when fewer and fewer people write checks?

o Offer seminars, workshops, and retreats that help people deal with excessive debt, financial planning, estate planning, or preparing wills.

o Offer classes or other gatherings where the focus is on giving as a spiritual discipline and teach people ways to cope with the risks of a materialist and consumerist society.

o Offer support groups for people struggling with bankruptcy, compulsive gambling, or unemployment.

o Launch communities and neighborhood gatherings for people who want to cultivate practices of simplicity, socially conscious investing, and environmental responsibility.

o Pastors and other leaders should adapt and improve their methods of communication and teaching about giving. Attend workshops, read the literature, use consultants, study scripture, learn about social trends and patterns of giving, and collaborate with other churches. Commit to these activities in order to learn new techniques and, more important, deepen theological understanding of giving, foster the charitable impulse, and inspire philanthropy. Make talking about money something natural rather than awkward.

o   Provide opportunities for people to learn about legacies, bequests, endowment giving, and estate planning. Invite people to consider supporting the church in their wills and estate planning.

o   Make legacy giving easy, providing information and means for people to prayerfully name the church as beneficiary of special gifts.

o   Make in-kind giving easy, providing information and means for people to donate investment shares, automobiles, and other property.

o   Express appreciation, regularly and in writing, for those who include the congregation in their estate planning.

o   Pastors should develop a comfortable willingness to initiate conversations with long-term attenders about planned giving.

o   Run quarterly reports of giving, and share them in a confidential manner with givers, to keep them informed in positive and consistent ways about their pledges and other giving. Make sure the report carries a tone of appreciation, a reminder of the significant difference the donor's gift makes, and a focus on the mission of changing people's lives. Include pictures of ministry activities so people can see how their contributions make a difference.

o   Pay attention to detail. Communicate clearly and concisely. Maintain financial records with great care for confidentiality and accuracy.

o   When people inquire at the church office or with the treasurer about their giving records, ensure that responses are quick, positive, and accurate, but never defensive, confusing, or delayed.

o   Take extraordinary precautions to protect the integrity of your financial systems by providing proper checks and balances for those who handle money, preparing regular and accurate financial reports for leaders and for anyone who requests them, and furnishing annual audits to appropriate financial officers.

o   Operate with transparency, knowing that trust is the currency of financial leadership and that confidence in the motives and competence of staff and volunteers is essential to cultivate giving. Pastors and designated leaders should know financial details, cash balances, giving patterns, and budget and should be able to communicate thoroughly and accurately about the congregation's financial health.

Habits That Help

Pastors, staff, and leaders speak in spiritual terms about the place of wealth, affluence, acquisition, materialism, selfishness, generosity, and giving. They do not avoid major capital funds campaigns, and they enter into major projects with excellence, professional preparation, and outstanding communication. They regularly offer people the opportunity to support special appeals and new projects, knowing that giving stimulates giving; and they've learned that when special giving is aligned with the purposes of Christ, it does not diminish support for the general budget. They encourage charitable contributions and philanthropic giving to community-service agencies and to cultural, medical, and advocacy causes that make a difference in lives of people.

Extravagantly Generous churches do more than encourage personal generosity, they practice generosity as a congregation, demonstrating exemplary support for denominational ministries, special projects, and missions in their community and throughout the world. They take the lead in responding to disasters and unexpected emergencies. Everyday disciples and pastors view "giving beyond the walls" as indispensable to Christian discipleship and to congregational vitality. They look for more and better opportunities to make a positive difference. They develop mission partnerships; support agencies that help the poor; and fund mission teams, scholarships, service projects, new church starts, and other ministries that transform people's lives. They make the mission of Christ real, tangible, and meaningful. Their reputation for generosity extends into the community.

Many churches do not have enough money because they don't provide sufficient ministry and mission. Rather than becoming obsessed with income, survival, and maintenance, they must continually return their focus to changing lives, reaching out to new people, and offering significant mission. By growing in ministry, giving increases.

In churches that practice Extravagant Generosity, the pastor tithes. Proportional giving with the goal of tithing, regardless of income, becomes an expectation for those who serve on the finance committee and in other key leadership roles of the church. The spiritual maturity that comes from growth in giving and the extraordinary engagement that results from tithing bring clarity of purpose and greater integrity to all the church's ministries.

The practice of Extravagant Generosity is the fruit of maturation in Christ, the result of God's sanctifying grace that molds our hearts and changes our values and behaviors. Generosity supports the other four practices, helping the church fulfill its ministry to make disciples of Jesus Christ in robust and fruitful ways, opening the message of God's love in Christ to more people now and for generations to come.

CONVERSATION QUESTIONS

How has someone else's generosity touched you and shaped your practices of giving? From whom did you learn generosity? Who continues to influence you toward greater generosity?

What's the most fun you've ever had giving money? What made the experience delightful, memorable, and meaningful?

GROUP ACTIVITY

Have people list what they perceive to be the four most important core values of the congregation—the essential and enduring tenets that are so fundamental that they must be kept no matter what the circumstance. Then list the four most dominant values of American culture as reflected in media, television, movies, magazines, advertising, business, celebrity culture, sports, politics, and fashion. Talk about how these contrasting values influence decisions about money, giving, and faith.

Chapter Seven

Fruitfulness and Excellence

"My Father is glorified by this, that you bear much fruit and become my disciples." (John 15:8)

In August 2006, Margie Briggs received a phone call from a district superintendent. Two small rural congregations had lost their pastor. He asked Margie, "Can you just get them through Christmas?" Thus began a story of renewal for two Missouri churches, Calhoun and Drake's Chapel.

Margie grew up in The Methodist Church, was formed by long-time service in United Methodist Women, and offered her gifts to her own congregation as well as to the larger connection. She was fifty-eight years old when she agreed to the few months of service as lay minister.

Step by step, the Calhoun congregation began to make changes, first in its space and then in its worship, its sense of community and purpose, and its outreach. The roof was replaced, the sanctuary windows renovated, a welcome area created. Two tiny restrooms became a single comfortable facility. The down-to-earth, thoughtful sermons and Margie's humility and graciousness drew people to worship, including many who had never stepped inside the church.

Drake's Chapel invited everyone in the community to an ice cream social. Fifty children and adults sat in folding chairs on the parking lot under the tall trees. Relationships were formed, and neighbors met. This congregation led the community to gather funds to support an individual undergoing cancer treatment who did not have insurance. As she formed relationships, Margie became the pastor of the whole community, and she was invited to lead funerals for people with varying faith backgrounds who had no connection to either church.

They also looked beyond worship, recognizing the toll rural poverty took on their community. Families lived on the edge, with poor pay and uncertain jobs. The congregations established a food pantry that anyone in need could access without shame. The Calhoun congregation invited all the children of the community to a party to hear the Christmas story and then to pick out gifts that had been purchased and wrapped by members. Someone suggested providing gifts to grandparents who didn't have the resources to give their grandchildren gifts. One year, more than seven hundred gifts were bought, wrapped, and given away.

Year by year, both churches grew as they experimented with any number of ideas to serve the communities. Drake's Chapel held an Easter sunrise service outdoors in the rolling hills. A musician with a lifetime experience of playing in bars started attending the Calhoun church. He composed songs based on the sermon theme. Worship came alive.

Unlike many small, rural communities, Calhoun and Drake's Chapel sought out ways to increase diversity. Sometimes, this meant just giving believers a chance to interact with those who live in a different context. Margie spoke with a pastor of an urban African American congregation in Detroit. A youth team from the Detroit church came to Calhoun to do a service project. Local people gathered cots, worked with a school for accommodation, identified projects such as rebuilding steps for homes of the elderly, and hosted the youth from Detroit. The following year, four youth and two adult sponsors—one who was seventy-three years old— traveled to Detroit for a mission trip, and so they experienced what the urban life is like for their friends.

A passionate layperson, two congregations willing to try new things, a vision for forming relationships and serving others—these led to renewal. During the ten years after Margie agreed to help out until Christmas, the Calhoun church celebrated sixty baptisms, sixteen affirmations of faith, and thirty letters of transfer. Drake's Chapel had eight baptisms and fifteen transfers (see Margie Briggs, *Can You Just Get Them through Until Christmas?* Cass Community Publishing House, 2017).

Los Naranjos (The Orange Trees) in McAllen, Texas, is an outreach ministry of El Divino Redentor United Methodist Church located north of Mission, Texas, in a *colonia* that goes by the same name. (A *colonia* is a low-income, rural, unincorporated community with mostly substandard housing along the US border with Mexico that frequently lacks basic infrastructure, such as paved roads, electricity, potable water, and proper drainage.)

The ministry was launched in 2010 after Fidencio and María Rodríguez, newcomers to El Divino Redentor, felt they needed to spread the Word of God in the community where their home is located. They had begun to follow Christ after Fidencio's near-death experience. Pastor Javier Leyva visited with the couple about what they might do, and an idea was born. The Rodríguez family would offer their home itself for ministry to the Los Naranjos *colonia*.

Another couple from the El Divino Redentor congregation agreed to lead the project. Jeremiah and Maggie Gutiérrez, were committed disciples,and got right to work, collaborating with the Rodríguezes. Their first step was to design an event for children. They knew parents would attend or at least be present before and after the event, which created the opportunity to invite parents and kids for upcoming dinners and worship services. The Saturday of Easter weekend was a strategic choice for scheduling the event.

That Saturday launched the faith community at Los Naranjos, which began meeting monthly in front of the Rodríguez trailer home, the worshipers gathering under a carport. Other disciples from El Divino Redentor joined the effort, and eventually the congregation's mission teams helped replace the Rodríguez family's trailer with a small home. A covered worship area was constructed in back of the house, sharing space with the family's washing machine and clothesline. Los Naranjos meets every second and fourth Saturday. People share meals at folding tables, children play in the small yard, a praise band projects slides against the back wall of the house, and worshippers pass insect repellent around to keep mosquitoes away.

Jeremiah and Maggie Gutiérrez and Rev. Nydia Jara organize and lead the gatherings. And the Rodríguezes have become leaders within the *colonia*, a key reason for the success of this ministry, which has expanded beyond the regular worship and dinner events. Mission teams repair homes and replace those that are uninhabitable. This ministry takes the love of God beyond the four walls of the church and into the community with no expectation of people traveling to El Divino Redentor. And yet many people who belong to the Los Naranjos community make the fifteen-mile trip to the church to worship on Sundays. El Divino Redentor has also launched other similar ministries—Los Ebanos, Kerygma, and Pan de Vida—under the leadership of Pastors Leyva and Nydia Jara, adapting the model to the surrounding communities.

The fruit of Los Naranjos? God is forming new disciples and is building relationships between the *colonia*, El Divino Redentor, and the people who serve through mission projects. Families who were living in the *colonia's* horrid conditions have more of life's essential resources, like safer housing and food. They have the chance to experience the hope and love of Christ. God is transforming not only the lives of those who participate but the *colonia* itself.

Leander United Methodist Church had been a traditional rural community for most of its 160-year history. In recent years, the city of Austin grew so quickly that Leander looked up one day and realized it was now a suburban church! Through the leadership of their pastor, this congregation saw the changing community around them as a missional opportunity instead of a threat.

Pastor Ray Altman and his family covenanted with a few other families to be in mission in their own neighborhoods. They shared a desire to become more missionally and incarnationally minded. The New Wineskin Initiative began with the leaders studying an eight-week primer on making mission more tangible and read a book about a church as movement. They practiced good neighboring more intentionally, following concepts gleaned from *The Art of Neighboring*. They formed relationships with neighbors they knew and those they had never met by visiting spaces where people gather, such as barbecues, dog parks, block parties, or trivia night at the bar. When such spaces did not exist or were difficult to enter, they created opportunities where neighbors could hang out and get to know one another.

Those who committed themselves to the initiative stayed engaged during the lengthy time frame required to form and grow authentic relationships. Through these relationships, they prayerfully sought to discover what God was up to and to honor and join the Spirit of God already at work in the lives of neighbors. Sometimes viable results took months. The process of discovery and relationship-building takes time. They asked questions, listened, and approached their calling with humility.

A few members began hosting parties in a neighborhood park. Neighbors, most of whom do not attend a church, help lead by bringing ideas, friends, and food. These gatherings strengthen neighborhood connections, forge friendships, and bring blessing. They foster a community of people who are committed to their neighborhood and its well-being and who grow in friendship together.

After about ten months of parties, Ray's family and others started hosting a potluck dinner twice a month where neighbors of different faiths (or with no faith at all) could talk about life, hopes, and dreams, and share in prayer. The potlucks provide a stepping stone between the low-threshold social space of the parties and the higher threshold space of discipleship formation.

"We assume that the kingdom of God has come near and is entering the world—both through the traditional church and outside of it," Altman says. "We assume that God is present and active in the people and communities outside of the church. We assume that most people in our communities are not interested in traditional church. We continue to do traditional church well and improve it for those who are looking for it, but we also learn how to do new things for people who are not. We assume that most people in our communities are open to faith, God, and to communities of faith. Prevenient Grace teaches us that God is already drawing people, even those who don't believe, toward Christ. We assume that God's image is present in all people outside the church and that we have something to discover about the Kingdom from them. To contain ministry in a church building is to miss the powerful work Jesus is doing in the world. We assume that God sends us to "go" from the church into the world to join in this work. This is the call of all followers of Jesus, not just missionaries or preachers. The Holy Spirit empowers all Christians to join in that work. People learn how to do this not in a study or sermon but from practicing it together in their neighborhoods and networks."

The Leander congregation evaluates the fruitfulness of the New Wineskin Initiative by focusing on the following question: Are we making disciples of Jesus Christ who are prepared for and active in incarnational mission? They measure how many people they are training, equipping, and sending into their neighborhoods and networks. They attend to relationships: Do people learn their neighbors' names, stories, gifts, and needs? They pray regularly. They find ways to join God's presence and work through serving.

Each neighborhood faith community trains a new leader for a year and sends them to start their own groups so that communities take root in new places. Leaders track each stage of development: discerning when to initiate a community, forming the Disciple Core Team, launching a new disciple core, training future disciples.

Another fruit of the initiative is transformed communities, guided by the question, "How is the kingdom coming in this neighborhood as it is in heaven?" Leaders measure participation of those unaffiliated with the church. They track acts of service, material improvements, needs identified and met. They watch for signs of reconciliation, healing, and love within the community. They listen for stories of transformation.

Stories abound of lives changed as a result of the initiative. People who previously never knew one another now give and receive spiritual and relational support during times of grief, loss, illness, or tragedy. Neighbors watch over one another with love. Folks who have felt alone now feel that their lives are interwoven with those of other people. Barriers and suspicions have been overcome. For many, the times spent at a dinner, a dog park, or at a party in the company of others who care for one another, pray for one another, and learn and serve together become the highlight moments of their month.

The New Wineskin Initiative has changed how the congregation understands its mission. As people see themselves as missionary disciples, they become more attentive to engaging in ministry not merely at the church campus but anywhere they connect with people.

The Conversion of the Imagination

The Conversion of the Imagination is the title Richard Hayes chose for his book on the Letter to the Ephesians (Eerdmans, 2005). No phrase better describes what has taken place in the faith communities described above. By the power of the Holy Spirit, pastors and everyday disciples underwent a conversion of imagination. They looked at their congregation's current ministries, the community around them, the contemporary attitudes of people who will likely never step through the door of a church, the mission of Christ and their role in that mission. The leaders and pastors began to see through different eyes. They made the shift from *come to us* thinking to *go to them* strategies, from *welcoming the stranger* to practicing locally rooted presence that requires *becoming the stranger*. They made the leap from attractional assumptions to missional assumptions.

If new life, fresh purpose, and greater fruitfulness can come to faith communities like Calhoun and Drake's Chapel in Missouri, Los Naranjos along the border, and Leander, Texas, it can happen anywhere. Each congregation became a center of missional preparation, a hub with spokes extending far beyond the church's walls to form communities and offer ministries in unexpected places.

Imagine your faith community developing ministries such as these.

How might a conversion of the imagination change you?

These are not churches that are going off the map. Rather they are following a map they never realized existed. The leaders experimenting with outreach into neighborhoods are not entering unknown and uncharted territory; they are stepping into communities unfamiliar to them but known and understood by people they have not yet met who live and work and play in those spaces. To move from mere attractional assumptions to more missional strategies we need help from people who can show us how to navigate. Interestingly, those navigators are usually people we have failed to even see before. And it must start with relationship, as we begin to experience life with those navigators—the people who are everywhere around us, where we work, live, and play. People who may never have been and may never come to our church.

The greatest threat to our mission today is not failing to offer ministry in an exemplary way but failing to experiment with new approaches. It's no longer true that we can just do things well and it will work, and people will come to our church. To do ministry requires a conversion of the imagination.

Creating new spaces for ministry requires experimentation. We listen. We learn. We form relationships. We fail sometimes, and then try a different approach. We look for how God is already at work in a neighborhood or network, and then align our lives with God's purposes.

To fulfill the ministry of Christ, congregations must change and grow and adapt in ways that are purposeful, thoughtful, and faithful. Change is not easy. People do not fear change as much as they fear loss, the letting go of comfortable and familiar patterns, behaviors, and attitudes. Change for the sake of change or to preserve the institution is not sufficient. Change takes many forms, and each congregation must find its own path.

By repeating, deepening, expanding, and improving upon the five basic practices of congregational ministry, churches change and grow and learn. Pervaded by the purpose of making disciples of Jesus Christ for the transformation of the world, churches discover new life, readily giving up the patterns that have limited ministry and eagerly taking up those that invite people into relationship with God. They open themselves to being reshaped by God's Spirit, revived and reformed to serve the ever-changing contexts and needs of people. As they form relationships with new people who grow in faith and in the practice of love, congregations breathe anew with an invigorating, animating sense of confidence and future.

A NEW VOCABULARY

Many churches don't even have a vocabulary for describing Los Naranjos or the missional experiments of the Leander church. Is Los Naranjos a church? Are the people who attend members of the mother church that started the ministry? Are leaders called pastors, even if they have no clergy credentials? Does people's attendance count in the attendance reports of the sponsoring congregation?

Fresh Expressions is a name given to forms of church established primarily for the benefit of people who are not yet members of any congregation. These communities vary from a community garden, to pub groups with Bible study, to crock pot ministries in trailer parks, to dinner churches in homes. The mission is to reach new people in new ways and in new places. (See Fresh ExpressionsFl.org or read *Fresh Expressions* by Kenneth Carter and Audrey Warren [Abingdon Press, 2017].)

In many Methodist conferences in Latin America, the pastor's end-of-the year report records the number of members and attenders, and then asks for the *Puntos de Predicación*, the name and number of "preaching points" and the count of people who attend. Maybe Los Naranjos and the Leander home communities are "preaching points," where Christ meets people in communities where the people already gather.

What are the Fresh Expressions or *Puntos de Predicación* your congregation uses to reach people who may never cross the threshold of a church building?

Something Must Change

The majority of mainline Protestant churches in the United States are slowing declining. Many independent and nondenominational churches follow similar trends. The rising median age of membership, the increasing personnel and facility costs, and the declining attendance have reached a point where congregations no longer have the people or resources to radically change directions. Fewer young people are attending, and there are more people who have no faith affiliation at all even as they search for a deeper spirituality. The median age in many churches is thirty years higher than in the surrounding neighborhood and the ethnic mix in the congregation does not match that of the community where it is located. Most pastors have never served in congregations that have reported growth during their tenure.

Something must change. Congregations cannot continue to do what they have been doing and expect downward trends to turn around.

It's becoming more difficult for leaders to ignore the prescient words of John Wesley, who wrote in 1786, "I am not afraid that the people called Methodists should ever cease to exist in Europe or America. But I am afraid, lest they should only exist as a dead sect, having the form of religion without the power" ("Thoughts upon Methodism"). He could have been describing any number of denominations besides Methodism. Answers will not come in easy-to-use new programs, through quick fixes, or by adopting new slogans. Blaming, scapegoating, denying, justifying, or ignoring have not helped and are unlikely to provide positive outcomes. The most substantial threats to the church's mission do not come from the seminaries, the bishops, the complexities of the ordination process, the apportionment system, or the conflicts between traditionalists and progressives, although all these deserve careful attention if the church is to move toward a new future. The most significant threats come from the failure to perform the basic activities of congregational ministry in an exemplary way and to experiment with missional strategies that take the church's people and mission into neighborhoods and networks.

A congregational culture of genuine hospitality, authentic worship, meaningful faith development, life-changing outreach, and selfless generosity requires a profound change in attitudes, values, and behaviors for most churches. Change does not happen quickly or without pain. And yet there are hundreds, and perhaps thousands, of churches like El Divino Redentor, Leander, Drake's Chapel, and Calhoun that have experienced profound renewal and new life.

Churches can change. By the grace of God, churches can step out in faith in radical new directions. They can chart a future that is different from the recent past. Their ability to become fruitful congregations is directly related to their willingness to perform the five practices in a consistently exemplary way.

Fruitfulness

Radical Hospitality. Passionate Worship. Intentional Faith Development. Risk-Taking Mission and Service. Extravagant Generosity. These five practices are so critical to the fruitfulness of congregations that failure to perform them in an exemplary way leads to the deterioration of the church's mission. Ignore any one of these tasks or perform any of them in a mediocre, inconsistent, or poor manner, and the church will eventually decline, turn in on itself, and die away.

Fruitful congregations do not merely perform these practices adequately; they repeat them while constantly learning, improving, excelling, and experimenting. Fruitfulness, excellence, authenticity, and a missional mind-set characterize every ministry of the church. Fruitfulness as a metaphor for the fulfillment of purpose is deeply embedded in our faith history. The scriptures are full of stories about fields and harvests, vines and branches, stumps and shoots, trees and figs. These give us a language for understanding effective Christian leadership and provide rich images for learning about the outcomes and consequences of our faith aspirations, commitments, and work.

The expectation of fruitfulness begins in the first chapter of Genesis when God says to human beings, "Be fruitful and multiply." Human fruitfulness is response to God's bounteous fruitfulness in making the heavens and the earth and all that is within them. The expectation of fruitfulness extends to the last chapter of Revelation, in which the author describes a new creation with a river of life flowing through the holy city. On each side of the river is the tree of life with twelve kinds of fruit, producing fruit each month, and its leaves are for the healing of the nations.

In Matthew, Jesus describes a disciple's life in terms of fruitfulness. He says, "Every good tree bears good fruit, but the bad tree bears bad fruit. . . . Every tree that does not bear good fruit is cut down and thrown into the fire. Thus you will know them by their fruits" (Matthew 7:17-20). The difference a person makes stems from interior qualities of character, motive, and relationship to God.

Mark tells of Jesus feeling hungry, seeing a fig tree, and cursing its lack of fruitfulness (Mark 11:12-14). Luke records the parable of the farmer who scattered seeds across the ground. Some fell on rocks, some dried out, and some were choked by weeds, but those which fell on good soil grew, producing an abundant harvest. Jesus says, "Let anyone with ears to hear listen!" (Luke 8:8). Despite inevitable obstacles and failures, disciples work steadfastly and with hope, trusting the God of harvest.

In John's Gospel, Jesus describes the relationship between life in God and fruitfulness. "I am the vine, you are the branches. Those who abide in me and I in them bear much fruit, because apart from me you can do nothing. . . . My Father is glorified by this, that you bear much fruit and become my disciples" (John 15:5-8).

The disciples of Jesus bore much kingdom fruit. They healed, taught, and served. They confronted evil, sought justice, and acted with mercy. They offered God's forgiveness and proclaimed God's reign. They changed lives, carrying in their words and work the message of God's love in Christ, and forming communities of followers. The gift of the Holy Spirit was in them because they were connected to God through Christ. Life in Christ and fruitfulness are inextricably bound together.

John Wesley expected evidence of grace, gifts, and fruit in ministry. The early Methodist examination question, "Have they grace for ministry?" focused on candidates' knowledge of God's pardon and love, their desire for nothing but God, and their experience of the sanctifying presence of God. "Have they gifts as well as grace for the work?" led to consideration of candidates' natural abilities and acquired talents, their sound understanding and faculty for communicating justly, readily, and clearly.

"Have they fruit in their ministry?" was Wesley's way of probing effectiveness and evaluating what a person's work yields for God's kingdom. "Have they convinced or affected anyone, such that they have received the forgiveness of God and a clear and lasting understanding of the love of God? Is the person an instrument of God's convincing, justifying, sanctifying grace?"

Fruitfulness for congregations means fulfilling the mission and purpose God has given them. Are we fruitfully and faithfully allowing God to work through our community of faith to make a difference in the lives of people?

Despite the common use of fruitfulness in scripture, many people respond negatively to applying it to churches. They argue that ministry isn't reducible to objectively measurable results and that one can't quantify effectiveness in congregational life.

While fruitfulness cannot be reduced to numbers, nevertheless numbers are important. Numbers represent people—each number stands for a person who is old or young, married or single, new to the faith or long established, rich or poor, immigrant or citizen. Each is someone's son or daughter, brother or sister, father or mother, friend and neighbor. Each is a person for whom Christ died. In Christ, each is a brother or sister to every one of us. Each is a person searching for a life that matters. Each needs community; and each wrestles with hope and despair, joy and grief, life and death. Each has a story, a history, and a future that are infinitely important in God's eyes. God desires to have a relationship with everyone, and God has breathed life into faith communities in order to reach them. How do we know three thousand persons were added to the community of the church in the days after Pentecost? (Acts 2:41). Because someone thought it was important enough to notice and to keep a record for two thousand years! If numbers are not important, then people are not important.

Most people intuitively value growth in ministry. When today's disciples think about the future of their congregation, what do they hope their community of faith will look like fifteen years into the future? What would their church look like if their prayers and hard work came to fruition? Would the church have fewer people, fewer children, and no new people? Would the church be weaker, smaller, older, and ready to close? Of course not. Implicit in people's hopes and hearts is the desire to pass along the faith to others who come behind them. People yearn for their faith communities to be alive, thriving, full of young people, confident about the future, and making a difference in the lives of more and more people.

Congregations should not consider themselves failures if their numbers are not huge. God uses all sizes and shapes of faith communities to reach people. But faithfulness to God demands that churches become more invitational and more missional, more able to offer excellent ministry and be better equipped for sending people into their neighborhoods to form relationships that change lives.

Ministries that are declining or that reach the same people now as they did ten years ago should pause to ask why this is. With an awareness of the scriptural expectation of fruitfulness, they might ask themselves how they can change their practices to become more invitational and missional. How can they use their gifts to initiate other ministries that reach people wherever they are?

Occasionally someone says, "God desires faithfulness, not fruitfulness." Search the Bible with a concordance to check references to fruit, harvest, sowing, vines, and seeds. Fruitfulness is clearly expected of faithful followers of Christ.

Fruitfulness and faithfulness are not mutually exclusive. Jesus himself shows us that one can and should be both fruitful and faithful. The same man who feeds the masses and heals the sick also spends time alone in morning and evening prayer.

Not all churches can be equally fruitful, and not all fruitfulness looks the same. A bishop shared with me her perceptions of fruitfulness. She described how sometimes one climbs up the tree, shinnies out onto a limb, and reaches far out into the branches to get just one apple. Other times, one simply shakes the branches and picks up what falls. And yet other times, without ever touching the tree, an abundance of apples piles up at one's feet.

There are situations where every small step toward fruitful ministry in Christ's name comes slowly and with great effort, careful strategy, and high risk. There are other situations where the harvest is so evident that we should ask God's forgiveness for not having done more in a season of readiness.

Whenever he was asked about how his ministry was going, one pastor always answered, "It's hard, hard ground. It's really hard ground." A sister pastor, tired of hearing her friend blame the mission field for lack of fruitfulness, finally said, "Sure it's hard ground. It's hard everywhere, but this is the patch of dirt Christ called us to work."

What makes for hard, hard ground? Are there really places where fruitful ministry is actually impossible?

Fruitfulness takes many forms—the growing care for one another in a congregation given to conflict, the deepening faith of a community that matures in Christ together, the increasing effectiveness of a mission initiative that changes lives. Even in these contexts, growth can be discerned as people engage and involve others, and share with them the good news that God has met our highest hopes and deepest needs in Jesus Christ.

Is it fair to expect fruitfulness and to hold one another accountable for fruitful ministry? Is it fair to propose goals that explicitly express a desire to multiply and deepen ministry? Not only is it fair, it is also faithful and necessary.

The language of fruitfulness causes faith communities to become clearer about desired outcomes. When congregations are unclear about outcomes and objectives, they resort to measuring inputs, efforts, and resources to evaluate success in ministry. A congregation may consider itself as wonderfully successful with youth ministry. They justify their evaluation because they have a full-time youth director, great volunteers, an excellent gymnasium, flat-screen TVs in the youth room, a van, and a generous budget for youth trips. But what if only six youth attend? Suppose none of them learns to pray, becomes familiar with scripture, helps with worship, or serves on a mission project. The church is measuring input rather than fruitfulness to assess strength. Fruitfulness directs our focus to what we accomplish for God's purposes and corrects the tendency to congratulate ourselves for all the work, resources, and people we apply to a task while ignoring or denying that our efforts may be making little difference. Focusing on fruitfulness keeps us faithful to purposes and makes it more difficult to justify and defend ineffective or unproductive ministries.

Many churches pray to God for more people, younger people, and more diverse people (Lovett H. Weems Jr. *Circuit Rider*, March/April 2006). And yet we cannot ask God to do for us what God created us to do for God.

More people—If we believe that faith helps people grow in relationship to God and makes a difference in the world, why would we not hope that more people deepen their faith? I yearn for more people worshipping God in churches and homes, more people studying God's Word in classes and retreats, more people offering themselves in service and mission, and more people speaking out for justice on behalf of the vulnerable. My highest desire is that more people learn the stories of the faith and grow in their understanding and experience of forgiveness, compassion, and love and that more people feel the sustaining presence of Christ through times of joy, grief, decision, and hardship. I pray for more people to develop the qualities of prayerfulness, service, kindness, gentleness, and generosity.

This desire is unselfish; it is a purpose worth pouring our lives into. To yearn to develop more relationships with people in order to deepen faith does not make us fundamentalist, aggressive, strident, or intrusive. This is a desire for which our faith communities should be fervent, passionate, open, and unceasingly invitational. The teachings of Jesus are laced with imperatives: "Go . . . Tell . . . Teach . . . Do . . . Love . . . Follow . . . Welcome : . ." His words are gracious, respectful, and loving, but they are imperatives nonetheless. They leave little room for misunderstanding his urgency for us to serve on Christ's behalf by offering grace to more people.

Younger people—Imagine a faith community that decides reaching younger people is vital. If the task of rethinking ministry with younger people became the mission, the faith community would become intentional about adapting ministries and methods to become more relevant and helpful. They would invite younger people into ministry with them. They'd have much to learn. They'd go to where young people are and do the things that young people do. They'd listen. But would God have it any other way than for people to give hearts full of Christ's love to those in succeeding generations? Jesus reminds his disciples never to hinder the children as they seek him (Luke 18:16), and he warns those who cause little ones to stumble (Luke 17:2).

Are the systems and approaches of your faith community helping or hindering, welcoming or providing obstacles for young people?

A special focus on younger people does not deny or neglect ongoing ministries to people of all ages. Rather it draws attention to the fact that the populations most absent and least served are children, youth, and adults under forty. Most of these will not get involved with congregations that shape all their ministries to fit the needs of people already present, namely older adults. To reach younger people requires special effort, adaptation, and change.

More diverse people—So many congregations no longer match the communities they serve. One church discovered that nearly 10 percent of households in its community were headed by single mothers. But single moms composed only about 1 percent of the congregation. Knowing that gives a clear notion of how God might be calling that church to focus its ministry. The more a congregation distances itself from the community it serves, the more it turns in on itself and the smaller its impact. A faith community that focuses all of its energy on a shrinking sliver of the social spectrum eventually dies.

To reach more, younger, and more diverse people requires changing systems, practices, and attitudes. Faith communities must pour themselves into the task with extraordinary intention, energy, and creativity. They stop making excuses, break through complacency, and offer ministry that is radical, passionate, intentional, risk-taking, and extravagant. They perform the critical practices of hospitality, worship, faith development, mission and service, and generosity in authentic ways. Remember: If renewal can happen in rural Missouri, along the South Texas border, and in suburban Austin, it can happen anywhere.

Excellence

Vibrant, fruitful congregations also place a high premium on excellence. They do not settle for mediocrity, indifference, or a tolerable adequacy. In all five practices, they offer their best; they continually learn and improve and evaluate and adapt. They exceed expectations; outdo themselves in their enthusiasm for quality; and offer exemplary hospitality, worship, learning in community, service and mission, and generosity.

Aspiring to excellence is deeply rooted in our faith heritage. God did not create the heavens and the earth and say, "It's good enough." Rather, scripture describes God imbuing creation with superlatives: "God saw everything that he had made, and indeed, it was very good" (Genesis 1:31). People offer their best and highest because God has given the best and highest.

Paul leads readers into his masterful and eloquent chapter on love with the words, "And I will show you a still more excellent way" (1 Corinthians 12:31). Love of God and neighbor surpasses all other strivings.

In Philippians, we find the admonition, "Whatever is true . . . honorable . . . just . . . pure . . . pleasing . . . commendable, if there is any excellence and if there is anything worthy of praise, think about these things" (Philippians 4:8). Christians aspire to develop rich interior spiritual qualities and to reflect these in what they do.

Paul commends the Corinthian congregation for their excellence: "Now as you excel in everything—in faith, in speech, in knowledge, in utmost eagerness, and in our love for you—so we want you to excel also in this generous undertaking" (2 Corinthians 8:7).

In Paul's most direct appeal to excellence, he writes, "Since you are eager for spiritual gifts, strive to excel in them for building up the church" (1 Corinthians 14:12). Excellence strengthens the body of Christ.

Spiritual motivation for excellence does not derive from marketing strategies as it might in the corporate world, trying to outdo competitors to win customer loyalty, or striving to come out ahead while climbing over weaker rivals. Excellence is not about superiority, outranking others, or seeking recognition.

Excellence in ministry derives from the desire to offer our utmost for God's highest purposes. Excellence means to "live your life in a manner worthy of the gospel of Christ" and "striving side by side with one mind for the faith of the gospel" (Philippians 1:27). Pursuing excellence means cultivating the gifts of the Spirit in us and in others to the fullest to the glory of God. To value excellence means that we take seriously a sanctifying grace with outward fruit and that we accept the lifelong task of seeking a still more excellent way in all that we do for Christ.

In their book, *Resurrecting Excellence: Shaping Faithful Christian Ministry* (Eerdmans, 2006), Greg Jones and Kevin Armstrong describe excellence in ministry as something perceptible and palpable. It's not only seen in "bodies, budgets, and buildings," but also in many other forms: the number of people whose lives are shaped by worship, hearts changed through Bible study, and a community life rich in Christ. Excellence may be revealed in the number of mission and outreach projects that transform lives and in the power and presence of God reflected in signs of forgiveness and gestures of reconciliation (p. 5).

Jones and Armstrong ask, "Where is the presence and power of God being manifested in this congregation's life, in this person's life, in this person's pastoral leadership?" (p. 6). Do we see it in numerical growth, new programs, and outreach? In expanding stewardship or creating new spaces for ministry? Do we see it in the pastor's hard work of reconciliation among factions in a community, in a congregation's willingness to care for those who are dying, or in a community's persistence in resisting injustice? Excellence takes many forms.

We cannot settle for what Jones and Armstrong have called "mediocrity masquerading as faithfulness" (p. 23). Vibrant, fruitful congregations perform the five practices in exemplary ways because they keep repeating them, improving them, honing them, sharpening them, deepening them, and extending them. They never forget how important these practices are.

Aspiring to excellence and authenticity means church leaders look to the five practices and ask not only "Are we performing these activities?" but also "Are we fulfilling these in a manner worthy of the mission God has given us in Christ? Are we offering our best? Or settling for mediocrity?"

Changed Lives

When I was in the third grade, our family moved to Del Rio, a small town along the South Texas border with Mexico. Lutheran by heritage, we had attended the Methodist church in our previous community because it was conveniently located. My father worked on Sunday mornings, and my mother took care of my baby sister. So the first time we attended worship, my father, brother, and I went alone, stepping into a small evening service at First Methodist Church. People sang hymns from the Cokesbury hymnal, and the pastor gave a message followed by a time for silent prayer during which everyone came forward and knelt. The service was simple, and the people were friendly. They seemed eager to meet us, and they invited us back.

A few days later, two church members knocked on our door, and my parents invited them into our small living room. Dan Lloyd and Bill DeViney welcomed us to town and expressed their delight in our visiting the church. They met my mother, told her about the church nursery, and expressed the hope that she, too, would visit the church.

Our family began to attend worship, sitting in the balcony so that my parents would feel less self-conscious about their children. I hold fond memories from my childhood and youth—the communion liturgy about our not being worthy so much as to gather up the crumbs under the table, the choir singing "Hallelujah" from Handel's Messiah on Easter, a revival in which the visiting preacher called me by name from the pulpit. I remember the duty entrusted to me to collect the offering in the balcony, covered-dish suppers, slide shows about missions, and musicals that retold stories of the Bible. I was confirmed in the sixth grade and began to attend the youth fellowship. I helped with vacation Bible school and became the AV (audiovisual) expert. I attended retreats, camps, backpacking trips, and service projects, all of them supported by volunteer sponsors. The youth chopped wood on a cold December morning to deliver mesquite to poor families with wood-burning stoves, sang in nursing homes, and helped at a center for mentally challenged adults. We trick-or-treated for UNICEF, washed cars to support the American Cancer Society, and took turns planning youth programs. When I was about sixteen years old, the pastor preached a sermon on the call to ministry and handed me a brochure titled "Are You Called to Ministry?"

Through the years, my parents became more active, joining an adult Sunday school class, helping teach a children's class, serving on committees, helping with dinners. Their best friends were people they came to know through the congregation; and over the years, they surrounded friends during times of grief, attended countless funerals, and celebrated the baptisms and weddings of their friends. My father served on the committee that planned the annual stewardship campaign, and even chaired it once. In their retired years, my mother and father signed up for in-depth Bible studies and delivered food with Meals on Wheels.

The ministry of First United Methodist Church in Del Rio that changed my life and the lives of my parents and family was simple and basic: initiating contact and welcoming strangers; providing engaging and authentic worship; offering opportunities for children, youth, and adults to grow in the knowledge and love of God; providing channels for meaningful service in the community; and helping members grow in giving. But by such ordinary congregational activities done consistently well, God shaped our lives in remarkable ways.

My parents belonged to First United Methodist Church in Del Rio for more than thirty-five years. With hindsight, one can track their growing engagement and activity, the increased understanding of the faith, and the expanding sense of responsibility they felt for their community.

If someone extracted from my parents' hearts, minds, souls, and memories all the influences accrued from thirty-five years of congregational belonging, they would be entirely unrecognizable from who they are now. If someone could remove all the learning and growing that came to them through friendships, worship services, Sunday school lessons, Bible studies, church suppers, private prayers, and mission projects, I cannot imagine who they would be, how they would see the world, in what ways they would relate to their community, or how they would experience the meaning and purpose of life and death. They would be completely different people than who they have turned out to be.

The journey to faith that I've described is repeated millions of times in tens of thousands of churches. In congregations small, large, urban, suburban, and rural, and in wonderful and magnificently diverse ways, people are welcomed, hearts are changed, communities are formed, service is rendered, and people from all walks of life grow in grace and in the love of God and neighbor. God uses congregations to make disciples, form faith, transform lives, and change the world.

What a remarkable difference one congregation can make for the purposes of God in so many people's lives. Imagine the friendships formed, the sustaining grace discovered, the love given and received, the hope inspired, the joy found, the justice proclaimed, and the new life experienced in so many lives through just one single congregation.

The experience of my parents and our family is now rare. Fewer people live in a single community for thirty-five years or seek to become members of a church. Far fewer children grow up active in congregational life. More common is people stepping in and out of congregational engagement, growing in faith through experiences far away from church buildings, moving from one job and location to another in a manner that restarts the need for community connection. Remember the story of Fidencio and María at Los Naranjos? A single life-changing experience caused them to open their home and hearts to their neighbors and dedicate their lives to serving God. In only a few months they moved from being recipients of Christ's Radical Hospitality, to realizing a new purpose for their lives, to offering Christ's Radical Hospitality to others in a profound way. The path of discipleship takes many alternative forms.

Through ordinary practices done well over time, faith communities make extraordinary differences in the lives of people. Through basic activities that express the prevenient, justifying, and sanctifying grace of God revealed in Christ, faith communities fulfill their mission. Making disciples involves a continuing cooperative effort on the part of the Holy Spirit and the church to bring people into relationship with God and neighbor through faith in Jesus Christ. The principal way God draws people into relationship with one another and with God is through faith communities—housed in beautiful sanctuaries or formed over dinners at home. They are expressions of the body of Christ, the means through which God reaches people with the gift and demand of God's grace.

God changes lives through faith communities, and this places upon pastors and disciples the awesome and joyful responsibility of cultivating strength, health, clarity of purpose, and faithfulness so that the mission of Christ thrives. The exemplary and repeated practices of Radical Hospitality, Passionate Worship, Intentional Faith Development, Risk-Taking Mission and Service, and Extravagant Generosity are the time-tested, theologically sound, and effective means by which faith communities fulfill their mission with excellence and fruitfulness to the glory of God. These practices stir the church to unexpected renewal and expanded vision, just as they have for centuries. Congregations are called to change the world, not just keep their doors open. God works through faith communities to offer "the life that really is life" (1 Timothy 6:19).

CONVERSATION QUESTIONS

How would your church look if your congregation committed to performing these five practices with excellence? What would change? Who would be with you who is not currently in your congregation? What excites you about that? What scares you about that?

How would personally practicing these five practices with greater intentionality shape your own faith journey? How would they change your habits, values, and attitudes?